Advertising Careers

ALSO BY JAN GREENBERG

Theater Business

Theater Careers

JAN GREENBERG

ADVERTISING CAREERS

How
Advertising
Works
and the
People
Who Make
It
Happen

119456

HENRY HOLT AND COMPANY
NEW YORK

Copyright © 1987 by Jan Greenberg
Published by Henry Holt and Company, Inc.,
521 Fifth Avenue, New York, New York 10175.
Distributed in Canada by Fitzhenry & Whiteside Limited,
195 Allstate Parkway, Markham, Ontario L3R 4T8.

Library of Congress Cataloging in Publication Data
Greenberg, Jan W. (Jan Weingarten)
Advertising careers.
Includes index.
1. Advertising—Vocational guidance. I. Title.
HF5827.G73   659.1'023'73   86–19368
ISBN: 0-8050-0379-7

First Edition

Design by Kate Nichols
Printed in the United States of America
1 3 5 7 9 10 8 6 4 2

ISBN 0-8050-0379-7

To Lester, Kim,
and Polly

Contents

Contents

Contents

Preface

This book is about advertising—how the business works, how ads are created, and, particularly, what it is like to work in advertising.

In 1986, more than $100 billion was spent advertising goods and services just in the United States. And the business is expanding. Advertising's importance in marketing products and services is greater than ever. This is in no small part due to the fact that most consumer items and services are virtually identical in quality and function. Thus, brand and name differences are perceived, not actual. Advertising not only informs us that something exists but also bestows image and personality onto otherwise indistinguishable products and services.

According to the industry magazine, *ADWEEK*, a national survey reports that only 11.3 percent of those questioned agreed with the statement, "I like commercials." But even if we are loath to admit it, the vast majority of us are influenced by advertising. And, like it or not, it is everywhere—over radio and television, in magazines and newspapers, on strategically placed billboards along roads, in airport terminals, and on the buses and trains that transport us. Increasingly, advertising appears where it is least expected. Helicopters and small planes fly over crowded summer beaches, trailing signs to inform us about a radio special or a new ice cream flavor. Nowadays, advertisers can even direct messages to olfactory senses. A favorite magazine might just smell of Paco Rabanne.

The U.S. Marine Corps spends more than $19 million a year reinforcing its image as the elite branch of the U.S. armed forces. Ronald Reagan assembled a mini–advertising agency to develop the advertising for his successful presidential campaign, persuading some of the business's most respected practitioners to take leaves of absence from their agencies. McDonald's tells us that "It's a good time for the great taste" of its hamburgers. New York City's champion baseball team, the New York Mets, lures crowds with the slogan, "Baseball like it oughta be." Separated lovers "Reach out and touch," making long-distance pillow talk via AT&T. Lionel Richie confirms that "Pepsi's it" while Coke's Bill Cosby lets us know "It's a hit." Even California's Forest Lawn mortuary (probably qualifying for the bad-taste award of all time) responds to the September 1985 Mexico City earthquake with a full-page ad in the *Los Angeles Times* stating, "If, God forbid, L.A. is next, our commitment will remain unshaken," and assuring its readers that their loved ones will be buried "with the sensitivity and dignity that have been our hallmark."

Indeed, advertising is part of our culture. During the winter of 1986, hundreds of people attended a retrospective of American ads at New York's Cooper-Hewitt Museum, many actually singing along with commercials aired in a montage of old television spots. Commercials are as much a part of our memory as the music of our youth. Is there anyone who grew up in the 1950s and 1960s who doesn't remember such lines as Clairol's "Does she or doesn't she?" or "L.S.M.F.T.—Lucky Strike means fine tobacco"? With a little prompting, any three-year-old today could probably recite an extensive repertoire of current commercial jingles.

This book focuses primarily on the very large agencies that operate on an international as well as a national level because they are the prototypes on which all agencies, regardless of size, are based. In these pages, more than fifty people, ranging from agency heads to advertising fledglings, speak about their careers. Hopefully the book will convey a real sense of the atmosphere and day-to-day business of advertising in addition to information about how advertising happens.

A final note: It is not easy to get a job in advertising. But once people do break in, during the beginning years especially, they change jobs with a frequency that, to me, seems unique to the business (although publishing might be a close second). A number of people interviewed were concerned about client confidentiality and requested anonymity. But I would wager that at least half of those identified in this book will have changed positions in the time that has lapsed between preparation of this manuscript and actual publication.

PART ONE
The Advertising Industry

1

Agencies

Advertising is the business of persuasion. Advertisers hope to make their products or services more attractive to more people than those of their competitors. Advertising agencies represent clients who have either a product or a service to sell—planning, creating, and placing advertising in print and over broadcast media.

Although the modern advertising business has its genesis in the U.S., advertising is not new. There appears to have been a flourishing advertising business in the Roman Empire. Excavations of the cities of Pompeii and Herculaneum, both buried by an eruption of Mount Vesuvius in 79 A.D., have unearthed what were probably among the world's first billboards. Wall inscriptions touting one wine as "frenzy wine" and a local bathhouse as "good enough for Venus" have been discovered. Scriptores (sign painters) created and produced advertising for clients, including candidates for political office, one of whom is on record as accusing the competition of being "drunken stay-out-lates."

The roots of the U.S. advertising business took hold in the mid-nineteenth century as new technologies changed the economy from one based on agriculture to one based on manufacturing. With thousands of miles of newly laid railroad track providing a means of transportation, manufacturers began to produce competitive goods that were distributed quickly and efficiently throughout wide areas. For the first time, consumers were not limited to one locally produced soap or cereal grain but could choose from a selection of products that were basically the same except for brand name. These are called *parity products*. The goal of advertising, then as it is today, was to create a perceived difference among these parity products in the mind of the consumer and to motivate purchasing behavior as well.

Advertising became an essential part of doing business. A manufacturer wanted to motivate consumers to purchase his product over all the other similar ones. Advertising not only informed people about a good's existence but touted its supposed superior and unique qualities.

Newspapers were the media of the day, so merchants purchased newspaper space to advertise their products. However, most newspapers didn't maintain accurate circulation records, nor were advertising rates fixed. An advertiser not only had to negotiate rates with each individual newspaper in which he wanted to place ads but, once the deal was set, had no idea whether the rate was high or low in relation to the newspaper's readership. Until 1869, when George P. Rowell published the first edition of *Rowell's American Newspaper Directory*, there wasn't even an available list of U.S. newspapers and their circulation figures.

Enter a go-between, Volney B. Palmer, who is today often referred to as the nation's first "ad man." As the first of what were called "newspaper agents," Palmer set up shop in 1843 in Philadelphia. He represented newspapers to potential advertisers. If a merchant wanted to advertise, Palmer helped select the most appropriate newspapers and forwarded the advertising copy plus the payment for the space to the papers. In return for Volney's representation, newspapers paid him a commission amounting to 25 percent of the cost of purchased space.

Once accurate circulation figures were available, however, advertisers could themselves decide which newspapers offered value. The newspaper agent was no longer needed. One agent, N W Ayer, decided to offer his clients help in preparing their ads, something that had been done before, but not in a systematic way. His business became the nation's first advertising agency. N W Ayer is today the eighteenth largest agency in the United States.

Advertising today includes not only newspaper space but magazine space, television and radio time, direct mail, point-of-purchase displays, package design, special-market advertising, sales promotion, outdoor and display advertising, recruitment, yellow pages, and new types of consumer advertising made possible by computer and cable technology. According to the U.S. Department of Commerce, there are almost ten thousand advertising agencies in the United States, ranging in size from one-person shops to billion-dollar communication conglomerates with thousands of employees throughout the world.

TYPES OF AGENCIES

Agencies are frequently categorized by the types of accounts they handle:

- *General consumer agencies* handle products and services that consumers purchase. These agencies tend to be among the largest and are what most people think of when referring to advertising agencies. General consumer agencies service accounts that include package goods (products wrapped and packaged by a manufacturer, such as detergents, foodstuffs, over-the-counter drugs, tobacco, and liquor); automobiles; airlines; and fast-food outlets. These are full-service agencies that are devoted entirely to the marketing and selling of consumer goods and services.
- *Recruitment agencies* work with corporate and institutional personnel departments to help attract potential employees by creating and placing advertisements in newspapers and specialized publications.
- *Business-to-business agencies* advertise services and items that are used by businesses rather than individual consumers. They create advertising that usually appears in special trade publications.
- *Entertainment agencies* specialize in theatrical, arena, and movie advertising and promotion.
- *Financial agencies* service financial institutions such as banks, brokerage houses, and investment services.
- *Travel agencies* represent foreign tourist organizations, hotels, and other travel-related organizations. Airlines and other modes of transportation, though, tend to use general consumer agencies.
- *Medical agencies* handle specialized pharmaceutical and medical products in which the advertising is most often directed toward physicians, nurses, hos-

pital administrators, and other professionals in the medical field.

- *Political agencies* work with individuals aspiring to elected office and with public policy and lobbying organizations that desire to disseminate a point of view or opinion.
- *Direct-marketing agencies* create advertising material in which the client sells directly to the consumer, avoiding middlemen, wholesalers, or intermediaries. This is the fastest-growing segment of the advertising business and includes direct mail and telemarketing.

In addition to their specialty, advertising agencies are traditionally categorized by the amount of money they bill each year. Agencies are generally paid on a commission basis, receiving 15 percent of the cost of purchasing the print space or broadcast time on or over which advertising appears. Billings are the total amount of its clients' monies that an agency spends each year. "Large" agencies bill more than $15 million a year, "medium" agencies bill from $5 million to $15 million a year, and "small" agencies bill under $5 million.

Increasingly, agencies and clients are negotiating other billing arrangements. These include hourly rates, straight fees, retainers, and special fees for special projects. For this reason, the industry trade publication, *Advertising Age*, ranks agencies by annual income as well as billings. Under the commission system, agencies sometimes can't make a profit on certain accounts. The client may require more work than the agency can possibly get back in its media commissions for the client.

Of the $100 billion spent annually for advertising, most is funneled through the roughly sixty "large" advertising agencies. These are the agencies that make up "Madison Avenue," although they are not all located on that street. As midtown Manhattan commercial real-estate costs skyrocket, agencies are moving away from Madison Avenue, often to reconditioned buildings located on streets south of midtown Manhattan. Agencies are also not even necessarily in New York. Leo Burnett Co., which numbers McDonald's among its clients and has annual billings of over $1.8 billion, is located in Chicago. Ketchum Communications, with over $400 million in billings, has main offices in Pittsburgh. Chiat/Day, with billings of almost $300 million and a reputation for innovative work for Apple's Macintosh computer, is California-based. So, the term *Madison Avenue* has become like the term *Broadway*, used to describe theater in general, even though only a handful of theaters are actually located on Broadway.

Large agencies can have branches throughout the United States and abroad. Agencies expand both to handle clients whose business is located in specific cities (such as automobile accounts in Detroit) and to be in a better position to pursue potential accounts. A number of agencies have recently opened offices on the West Coast to be in a better position to sell themselves—or "pitch," as it is called in advertising parlance—for computer and high-technology accounts.

Although large urban centers tend to house the largest agencies, in the past few years agencies situated in smaller cities have received increasing recognition for their creative work. These agencies do not handle many clients who advertise on national television but they do prove that exciting and creative work is in no way limited to the largest agencies. Minneapolis's Fallon McElligott Rice was designated *Advertising Age*'s 1983 Agency of the Year. And in 1986, the *New*

York Times and *ADWEEK* cited regional agencies for their creative product; these included Livingston & Company (Seattle), Wieden & Kennedy (Portland, Oregon), Leonard Monahan Saabye (Providence), McKinney Silver & Rockett (Raleigh), the Martin Agency (Richmond), Goodby, Berlin & Silverstein (San Francisco), Mullen Advertising (Boston), Krause & Young (Dallas), and Carden & Cherry Advertising (Nashville).

AGENCY STRUCTURE: CORE DEPARTMENTS

Regardless of size, all agencies have the same goal—to create advertising that will sell the client's product or service. And all agencies are organized in the same way, although a large full-service agency is necessarily more structured and formal than a smaller agency, in which one person might wear many hats. For instance, in a smaller agency one person might oversee both the production of a radio spot and the purchase of the time over which it will be broadcast; in a large agency, these functions are handled by the production and media departments respectively.

Although agency departments will be fully profiled in the following chapters, here is a brief overview of agency organization. Keep in mind that, although all departments within an agency are interdependent, the actual work within each is specialized. People who work in advertising have different skills. A beginner in the business will most likely begin as an assistant in the department for which he is hired and will receive on-the-job training. So, if you are thinking about a career in advertising, it's a good idea to be clear from the beginning about what part of advertising interests you. Although there are, of course, exceptions, people do not routinely move from department to department.

Account Services Account executives are the agency's representatives to the client. They coordinate and are responsible for all agency work done for the client and must also make sure that the account is profitable for the agency.

Research Agency researchers plan and execute research projects that help identify the audience to whom the client directs the advertising. Researchers also test creative material to see whether it is effective in reaching the audience.

Creative Copywriters and art directors create the actual advertising product, which includes print ads for newspapers or magazines, display ads for outdoor billboards and public transportation, radio and television commercials, coupons, special mailings, and newspaper and magazine inserts.

Media Media planners decide where the advertising should be placed so that it will reach the desired audience. Media buyers purchase the print space and television and radio time.

AGENCY STRUCTURE: SUPPORTING DEPARTMENTS

Production Print production converts the artwork and copy into finished advertising. Broadcast production coordinates the entire process of commercial production from casting to the final mix, at which point the spot is ready to be aired.

Traffic Traffic coordinates and schedules all creative and production work and makes sure that all ads and commercials get to the right place at the right time.

Legal The legal department handles contracts and licensing agreements and makes sure that all advertising created by the agency is within the guidelines set by federal and state regulatory agencies. Those in commercial clearance work with the television networks to make sure that commercials are approved before they are accepted for broadcast.

Business Affairs The business-affairs department oversees all financial affairs, including client fees and billings, talent payments, and production costs.

These then are the standard departments in advertising agencies. Small agencies often use outside suppliers for such services as research or media buying. Large agencies frequently have additional departments that include new-product development, new business, international advertising, sales promotion, administration, personnel, and public relations.

2

The Business

People often use decades in describing advertising trends. The 1950s, the decade in which television became popular, are also known as the decade in which USP—the unique selling proposition—became the standard on which many agencies based their work. The term *USP* was coined by Rosser Reeves, cofounder with Ted Bates of Ted Bates Advertising. USP is based upon the premise that every product or service has a characteristic that makes it unique. The key to USP is to tell or show the consumer the one, clear benefit that the product or service offers—that quality that makes it different from any competitive product or service.

The fifties were the age of the hard sell and, according to Reeves, it didn't even matter if the consumer liked the ads. Under Reeves's leadership, the Ted Bates agency created commercials with such USPs as "Wonder Bread helps build strong bodies twelve ways" and "Colgate cleans your breath while it cleans your teeth." The idea was to drum the USP into the mind of the consumer. Commercials were often repetitive, brash, sometimes annoying—but by no means ineffective.

Typical was the ad that Reeves himself claimed, in a 1969 *New Yorker* profile, to be "the most hated commercial in the history of advertising." It was the commercial for Anacin showing three boxes inside the head of a man suffering from a headache. In these boxes an electric-shock mechanism, a coiled spring, and a pounding hammer dramatized the headache, which was cured by bubbles of Anacin traveling up to the man's head from his stomach. Hard-selling and harsh, the commercial worked. According to Stephen R. Fox's book on the history of advertising, *The Mirror Makers*, within eighteen months Anacin sales went from $18 million to $54 million.

However, during the 1960s, there was a reaction against this often humorless and irritating advertising. This was the decade that is sometimes referred to as the "age of creativity." Although the concept of USP has endured in advertising and is the premise behind many ads today, there arose in the sixties a sense that advertising could be amusing, perhaps even sophisticated, and still be effective. This was the period during which William Bernbach, one of the founders of Doyle Dane Bernbach in 1949, teamed copywriters and art directors together and set a standard for advertising that was stylish, witty, and entertaining.

The advertising business responded to the economic recession of the 1970s by becoming more conservative. Clients, concerned about expenditures, opted for safety over innovation. The account and research departments dominated agencies. Consumer research, and concept and copy testing, began to be widely used. Agencies assumed the role in which they continue today, of consultants and initiators in their clients' entire marketing process.

In the future, the 1980s may very well be viewed as a period in which technological development radically changed the business. Satellites and high-speed communications equipment now enable businesses and agencies to expand internationally, resulting in an emphasis on global rather than regional advertising. Computers enable marketers to identify consumer target audiences with an acuity and speed even a score of professionally trained individuals would find impossible to duplicate.

Technology has also made agencies and their clients rethink just how advertising dollars are best spent. VCRs and remote-control devices make it possible for consumers to switch television channels away from, or fast-forward through, unwanted commercials simply by pushing a button—"zap," as it is called in the business. Conventional television advertising is no longer necessarily cost-efficient for advertisers. Clients are utilizing technology to seek new and effective ways to present messages to consumers. Today's advertising agencies no longer simply produce and supply print, television, radio, or outdoor advertising and place it in the appropriate media. Rather, no matter what their size, agencies are, more often than not, involved with their clients' entire sales and marketing effort. Clifford Emery founded Emery Associates in West Hartford, Connecticut, several years ago with himself, a secretary, and "a very good group of independent free-lancers." He says:

"I think advertising agencies really do a terrible job of identifying what they do. Here we are in communications and we don't even say what it is we do. We are a sales agency. Advertising is only one of the things we can do to help sell goods. We help with public relations, direct mail, promotional sales incentives, training, and research."

COLLATERAL

Advertising that does not involve the traditional purchase of time or space in communications media is called *collateral*. Collateral represents the fastest-growing area within the advertising business. It used to be considered the stepchild of advertising. Small agencies, often in outlying suburban areas and without the prestige of traditional, mainstream agencies, handled collateral. This is changing. All agencies offer clients collateral expertise; many have actually purchased collateral businesses, bringing them into the agency fold. Other agencies have developed specialized collateral departments, staffed by savvy and creative advertising professionals.

A list of collateral services illustrates its prominence today. In general, agencies did not routinely offer these services until just a few years ago:

Direct Marketing

Direct marketing enables advertisers to sell directly to consumers. "Junk mail," Book-of-the-Month Club, record clubs, fund-raising appeals, and mail-order catalogues are all examples of direct marketing. Direct marketing is attractive to advertisers not only because it is usually less expensive than traditional advertising, but because it elicits an immediate and measurable response. Computers make it possible for marketers to maintain lists of potential customers and facilitate sophisticated segmentation in which direct marketers identify and separate specific potential buying publics.

Telemarketing is the fastest-growing form of direct marketing. In an *ADWEEK* interview, Rudy Oetting, president of Telephone Marketing Resources, comments, "People in the marketplace are a lot more attuned to verbal skills than they are to reading and writing. They are much more apt to pick up a telephone to do business."

Easily available credit cards and toll-free, twenty-four-hour "800" telephone numbers make it easy for consumers to order and pay for purchases. Even motion-picture companies promote films over the telephone. According to *Advertising Age*, when advertisements for the film *Ghostbusters* listed a toll-free number that fans could dial to hear messages recorded by stars Bill Murray and Dan Aykroyd, more than 225,000 people called each day.

Changing life-style patterns have also been influential. As most women now work outside the home, families may have more discretionary income but less time in which to spend it. Whereas companies like Sears, Roebuck formerly used mail-order catalogues to offer inexpensive and durable products to consumers who simply didn't have easy access to stores, today's mail-order companies, such as L. L. Bean and Land's End, use catalogues as a marketing tool especially directed toward groups to whom their products give prestige. The Spiegel catalogue now even offers designer clothing from the likes of Bill Blass, Laura Ashley, and Anne Klein.

Sales Promotion

Sales promotions are special incentives that are offered to encourage people to purchase a product or service while at the same time increasing its visibility in the marketplace. Promotions include coupons, contests, sweepstakes, and point-of-purchase displays designed to capture consumer attention at the place of sale. This is a fast-growing facet of the business. For example, *Advertising Age* reported that in 1982, there were 120 billion coupons distributed, an average of 1,400 per U.S. household. That was six times the number of ten years before. By 1984, the figure was almost 165 billion. Seemingly nonrelated businesses sometimes offer joint promotions, to the benefit of both. For instance, in 1985, there was a joint TWA and Polaroid promotion in which purchasers of Polaroid cameras received TWA certificates entitling them to a 25 percent fare discount within a fixed time period.

Special-Event Sponsorship

Advertisers subsidize events such as concert tours and sports events. In return, the advertiser's logo is prominently displayed on scoreboards, official T-shirts, and stadium billboards. Virginia Slims has long sponsored women's tennis tournaments and Jovan pioneered rock-concert sponsorship in 1981 when it underwrote the Rolling Stones tour. Pepsi recently sponsored Tina Turner, and Kodak appeared as a prominent sponsor of the 1985 Live Aid concert.

Public Relations/Publicity

Advertisers purchase time or space; publicists seek unpaid or free attention. Public relations is often used in conjunction with advertising to present a company, organization, product, or individual in a way that enhances public perception.

Publicists prepare speeches for company executives, arrange news conferences, write and distribute special features and stories, book television and radio appearances, and manage special events for clients. Dupont, to introduce a new synthetic marble look-alike product called CORIAN about fifteen years ago, had its publicists arrange a national tour for a "lady carpenter." Because her gender made her a novelty, Dupont publicists had no problem booking the lady carpenter on local television shows in cities throughout the nation, where she gave bathroom-renovation tips—using CORIAN, of course.

Coca-Cola's press representatives understood the importance of hype in handling the announcement of the soft-drink's reformulation in 1985. Its public-relations agency, Burson-Marsteller, announced the date on which a press conference would be held to discuss the "most significant soft-drink development" in the company's history—just before an August weekend, a notoriously slow time for news. With time on their hands, the press spent the entire weekend trying to figure out what the "development" was, and newspapers and television were full of advance coverage.

Public relations plays a more serious role as well. Recent tragedies such as the Tylenol poisonings, the gas leak at Union Carbide's plant in India, New Jersey's Great Adventure amusement-park fire, and the massacre of twenty people at a Southern California McDonald's all required careful public-relations strategies to handle corporate and public reaction. Burson-Marsteller even has a crisis communications group that was formed to counsel and help its clients during such emergencies.

One of the stranger public-relations problems has been Procter & Gamble's need to cope with on-again, off-again nationwide rumors associating the manufacturer with satanism. Starting in 1980, there were rumors that the P&G trademark was the mark of the devil. The trademark, showing the man in the moon and thirteen stars, had its origins around 1850 as a rough cross that was used by dockworkers to identify P&G's Star-brand candles. The cross evolved into a star and then, in 1902, a cluster of stars to represent the original thirteen colonies. According to P&G spokespeople talking to the *New York Times*, in 1920 the man-in-the-moon face was added just as a "popular fancy."

In 1985, however, the satanism rumors that had begun on the West Coast surfaced in the South and Northeast. Proctor and Gamble was deluged with telephone calls from people asking about its relationship with Satan. Procter & Gamble attempted to quell the rumors by setting up a toll-free telephone number that concerned people could call for information, hiring detective agencies to track down the actual source of the rumors, organizing press conferences, and drafting careful statements by Procter & Gamble spokespeople. However, in April 1985, the company, after consultation with its public-relations agency, Hill & Knowlton, decided to remove the trademark design from its products.

MERGERS AND ACQUISITIONS

Advertising agencies have responded in various ways to their clients' growing use of alternative and collateral services. Many of the larger advertising agencies buy smaller companies that offer the services or create those capacities themselves.

For instance, in the spring of 1985, Ogilvy & Mather International, the parent company of Ogilvy & Mather Advertising and other related businesses, changed its name to the Ogilvy Group, a name symbolic of the company's commitment to comprehensive marketing services for its clients. It announced the name change in a double-page ad that informed potential clients, "An outstanding advertising campaign should be the minimum requirement," and that "your agency should know how to speak with a dozen voices that sound as one—to any target audience, in any market or group of markets—locally, nationally, or internationally. In direct response, in sales promotion, on cable, in public relations, as well as in thirty seconds on television." To that end, the Ogilvy Group can call on divisions that handle advertising, direct response, promotions, public relations, graphic design, recruitment advertising, business-to-business advertising, and yellow pages.

This trend is a source of some concern to small agencies, which cannot easily offer the same services a large one can. Don Dickison, a former Ogilvy & Mather copy-group head and now co-owner of his own agency in Westport, Connecticut, says, "We have a public-relations arm, a direct-response arm, and a sales-promotion arm. The reason I did that was that the major agencies are doing it and we like to offer the same range of services a big agency does. We can't necessarily do it with the same depth, but we can certainly do it with quality."

In addition to purchasing related businesses, in the last five years many agencies have expanded by merging with one another or by acquiring other advertising agencies. From a few widely reported mergers in the early 1980s, such as Ted Bates's 1982 acquisition of William Esty for an estimated price of $50 million, merger fever has risen to the point where, in 1985 alone, the American Association of Advertising Agencies reported nineteen mergers. In 1986, there were already twelve by early May.

Agencies buy other agencies and merge for several reasons. As mentioned before, clients require an increasing array of services, today often including international capabilities. The trend is for clients to reduce the number of advertising agencies they use throughout the world, relying instead upon a select few that have international resources and can service them in the places in which they do business. A careful merger can, in addition, help an agency solve possible management or creative problems.

But mergers really provide a way for agencies to expand and grow, opening the way for increased profits for participating principals and stockholders. The *New York Times* reported, for instance, that when the April 1986 merger of BBDO International, Doyle Dane Bernbach, and Needham, Harper Worldwide—three of the world's largest agencies— was announced, one of the goals stated by Allen G. Rosenshine, chairman and chief executive officer of BBDO, was "to be nothing less than advertising's global creative superpower."

However, the BBDO/Doyle Dane Bernbach/Needham, Harper Worldwide preeminence, creating collective world billings of more than $5 billion a year, lasted less than three weeks. In May 1986, the British-based advertising agency Saatchi & Saatchi announced its acquisition of Ted Bates Worldwide. This culminated a buying spree that had begun in 1982 with the purchase of Compton Advertising and continued with the 1983 purchase of McCaffrey & McCall; the 1986 buy-out and merger of Dancer Fitzgerald Sample with Saatchi's own British agency, Dorland Advertising, to form DFS/Dorland; and the April 1986 acquisition of Backer & Spielvogel.

Saatchi & Saatchi's buy-out of Ted Bates Worldwide for a reported $450 million has created an advertising superpower with worldwide billings of over $7.5 billion. The Saatchi & Saatchi empire now includes (1) advertising: Saatchi & Saatchi Compton Worldwide, with ninety-two offices in fifty-four countries; McCaffrey & McCall, with three U.S. offices; Backer & Spielvogel, with two offices in the United States; DFS/Dorland Worldwide with forty-four offices in thirty-one countries; and Ted Bates Worldwide, with 104 offices in forty-seven countries; (2) six direct-marketing companies; (3) three sales-promotion companies; (4) five public-relations companies; (5) two graphic-design and corporate-identity firms; (6) one executive-recruiting company; (7) two management-consulting companies, with one, the Hay Group, represented by one hundred offices in twenty-seven countries; and (8) one of the world's largest market-research companies, Yankelovich, Clancy, Shulman (statistics from *Advertising Age*, July 7, 1986).

These mergers will have a profound, although as yet uncertain, effect on the advertising business. By mid-August of 1986, over two hundred people had been laid off by agencies involved in recent mergers, primarily the result of account shifts and losses. Those most affected were middle-level account personnel and indications are that the employment picture for account executives will continue to be sluggish.

In addition, these mergers have generated a lot of discussion within the business about the nature of advertising in general. Questions have been raised as to whether a consortium of merged agencies can overcome the rigidity endemic to large corporations and offer clients the flexibility and individual attention so important in developing creative advertising.

Capitalizing on these concerns, J. Walter Thompson, the large, international but as yet unmerged agency, took the opportunity to stress its single, unmerged status in a newspaper ad. With a headline that read, "J. Walter Singular," the ad called attention to the fact that six of its campaigns had made the Video Storyboard Tests' 1985 list of the ten best-liked campaigns, whereas BBDO, NHW, and DDB together had managed only three.

However, there have also been moves in the opposite direction. McCann-Erickson recently created an agency within an agency, operated by McCann's two executive vice-president/creative directors, Ira Madris and Bruce Nelson. Called Ira Madris, Bruce Nelson & Colleagues, the agency is a high-priced boutique for clients who are willing and able to pay for the attentions of the creative duo throughout the entire advertising process. And in early 1986, Roy Grace, chairman and executive creative director of Doyle Dane Bernbach, formed a new agency with Diane Rothschild, also of Doyle Dane Bernbach, called Grace and Rothschild. Observing that "the irony in a large agency is that the better you are at what you do, the more likely you are to rise to a level where you no longer do it," Grace told *ADWEEK* that he plans to serve no more than ten clients at a time.

CONFLICTS

These mergers make the problem of client conflict increasingly complicated. An advertising agency cannot handle accounts with identical or even similar products. For instance, an agency won't handle competing sugar-free soft-drink accounts or dried-cat-food products. The rationale behind that is obvious. No manufacturer wants an agency divided in its effort to create the best advertising for his product. In addition, businesses are reluctant to disclose confidential product information to people who might, however unconsciously, use that information to benefit its competitors.

To get around this, the super agencies created by recent mergers operate as holding companies retaining separate agencies, each under independent management. For instance, Ted Bates operates as an autonomous agency under the Saatchi & Saatchi umbrella; and Doyle Dane Bernbach and Needham, Harper formed one agency, DDB Needham Worldwide, with BBDO remaining separate. All have become part of the newly created Omnicom Group's family of agencies.

The idea of holding several independent advertising agencies under one corporate umbrella originated with Marion Harper, who, as president of McCann-Erickson, was responsible for that agency's meteoric success in the 1950s. In 1960, Harper created Interpublic, one of the nation's first communications conglomerates. By 1966, Interpublic was the largest organization in the world devoted to marketing communications. Interpublic owned and operated ten advertising agencies and twelve companies that specialized in sales promotion, research, public relations, and other marketing services.

Of most interest to Harper, however, were the Interpublic member advertising agencies. Each was autonomous with separate personnel, offices, and clients. As part of the Interpublic group, but as separate entities, these agencies could service a multiplicity of accounts, including several brands within the same category, a situation that would have been a conflict within a single agency. However, under Harper, Interpublic became a Frankenstein monster, created by genius but growing out of control. Questionable business practices and financial difficulties finally resulted in Harper's dismissal by his own board of directors.

Interpublic still exists as the holding company and financial management group for its four independent advertising agencies: McCann-Erickson, Marschalk Campbell-Ewald, SSC&B:Lintas Worldwide, and the Los Angeles–based Dailey & Associates. To avoid any potential conflict problems, Interpublic has a policy that agency personnel can move from one agency to another only after approval by all parties who might be concerned.

Although the issue of possible conflicts might seem fairly obvious, what actually constitutes a conflict is not always clear. It is often a subjective decision on the part of a client. Hallmark decided a conflict existed when its agency, Young & Rubicam, took on AT&T as a client. Hallmark's rationale was that at certain times of the year, particularly Mother's Day and Easter, advertising efforts to get consumers to buy and send greeting cards were in potential conflict with advertising to get consumers to make long-distance telephone calls. Ogilvy & Mather now handles Hallmark.

Sometimes agencies themselves drop clients in order to avoid conflicts. This usually happens when one client has the potential to generate greater billings than the other. At the time of its merger with Doyle Dane Bernbach and Needham, BBDO resigned an estimated $80 million in media buying for Stroh Brewery Co. and Old Milwaukee beer, so as not to jeopardize Needham's more than $100-million Anheuser-Busch business (which included Michelob Light, Bud Light, and Busch beer). The resignation made even more sense because Needham planned to pursue additional Anheuser-Busch work held by Ted Bates. Needham was successful and was awarded the $50 million Michelob account.

But more often clients make the first move. By mid-August of 1986, over half a billion dollars in client billings had been switched and reassigned as a result of mergers and acquisitions. Needham, Harper Worldwide lost $58 million in American Honda business to the Los Angeles–based agency Rubin/Postaer & Associates because BBDO services Chrysler while DDB has Audi and Volkswagen. Ted Bates Worldwide lost over $300 million in billings including $80 million from Colgate that went to Young & Rubicam and Foote, Cone & Belding, two large but unaligned agencies, and $34 million in Warner-Lambert business that was assigned to J. Walter Thompson ("J. Walter Singular"). These clients all

119456

were concerned about direct conflicts with rival businesses that have accounts at Saatchi & Saatchi.

It is rare that clients and agencies make the smooth transition that occurred when Grey Advertising acquired a majority interest in Levine, Huntley, Schmidt & Beaver in July 1985. Hailed as a milestone in client acceptance of conflicts, the merger announcement stressed each agency's continued independence, and spokespeople stated that client approval had been secured before final papers were signed. The agreement was needed because Levine's client roster included Subaru, and Grey had Renault; Levine had Citizen Watch, and Grey had Timex; Levine had Konica, and Grey had Canon; and Levine had Kronenbourg beer, while Grey had San Miguel.

NEW BUSINESS

According to a special March 1984 *ADWEEK* supplement, with the average life of an account for an agency only two to four years, and more than five hundred major advertisers switching agencies each year, agencies continually pursue new business. Agencies even advertise themselves, as in the Ogilvy Group ad portraying the agency as a full-service marketer. J. Walter Thompson has appealed to businesses concerned about the number of people who actually watch television commercials with an advertisement citing figures that show its ads to be the least frequently "zapped." These ads appear most frequently in the advertising trade publications *ADWEEK* and *Advertising Age*, and national business newspapers including the *Wall Street Journal* and the *New York Times*.

Attracting new business has gotten very complicated and

expensive for agencies. Years ago, an agency got new business simply by showing the creative work it had previously produced. Agencies today often spend thousands of dollars in time, manpower, and materials pitching new business once they know that a client is interested in their agency. Some agencies expect their research, account, creative, and media teams to spend roughly 20 percent of their time on new business. And a few agencies have researchers who work fulltime on new business possibilities.

Large agencies have new-business teams, usually composed of senior personnel, who meet regularly to discuss potential clients. Even before a company publicly announces that it is making its account available for review by agencies, most large agencies have a pretty good idea that the account will be up for grabs. Agencies constantly monitor the advertising and performance of potential clients in the marketplace and are highly attuned to any rumor of client dissatisfaction with its current agency. By the time a client publicly announces an agency review, competing agencies frequently will have spent hundreds of man-hours devising a strategy and presentation to appeal to the prospective client.

Agencies more often than not do speculative work for potential clients. Speculative work includes sample print ads and storyboards; sometimes the agency actually produces a television commercial (often using agency personnel as actors). It's very expensive, and only a rare client is willing to pay for speculative work.

Such work is particularly difficult for smaller agencies. "I spend about twenty percent of my time on new business," says Don Dickison. "Sometimes a client will pay us for new-business presentations, but that's rare. I think speculative work is a disaster. You have a staff of people to service the existing clients. If you organize your office right, your staff is fairly lean and every one of them is busy. And then you get a new-business presentation dumped on you, and everyone works on it. It puts a big burden on the agency, and it's a real anticlimax when you don't get it. And you usually get about one out of ten."

In November 1984, when J. Walter Thompson won the $68-million Miller High Life account after an eight-month, eight-agency review, one Thompson copywriter commented that everybody seemed to have worked all summer on the Miller pitch. As one researcher at a large agency says, "We usually don't spend a lot of money on research until we know that the client is interested in talking to us. Often the account group does a quick situation analysis with information on product sales. They will ask us to come up with information on the consumer and what kind of segments exist in the market. The client is often so overwhelmed by the work we've done, and the results and data, that they take us on—if they agree with the direction."

Agencies do some outrageous things to get new business. When it was pitching *People* magazine, Geer, DuBois got Liv Ullmann to sit in the receptionist's seat when *People* representatives came to visit the agency. The Bloom Agency, competing for the WABC-TV account, installed a large blow-up of the Bloom creative team in a bus shelter directly opposite the station's New York offices in a parody of the WABC-TV advertising campaign featuring a photograph of the ABC newscasters, with the headline "Here's the team." (As it happened, neither agency got its accounts.)

When N W Ayer was pitching the J. C. Penney Company account with its approximately $60 million in billings, it went beyond preparing an effective advertising strategy along with samples of possible commercials; when J. C. Penney executives arrived at the Ayer audiovisual center for the presentation, they found the foyer decorated with J. C. Penney items and the center itself a mock-up of Penney windows.

Once an agency gets the business, the next challenge is to keep it. Obviously, an agency that doesn't produce satisfactory work for a client won't keep the account. But success in the business requires more than just good advertising material. Most people agree that the most important thing in making a client/agency relationship work is chemistry and personality. "Chemistry," says Don Dickison, "is ultimately the most important thing between a client and an agency. It takes time to develop a relationship. You can't hit the ball over the fence on the basis of one or two meetings."

Ted Bates's senior vice president/management supervisor Jerry Brady says, "Clients and agencies might often have different points of view, but all have the same objectives. If you work together with that understanding and spirit, you can have a lot of honest disagreement and make progress. A good client is not an easy client. That's not a definition. A good client is demanding, positive, fair, and supportive."

As Jay Chiat, the president of Chiat/Day, wrote in *ADWEEK*: "We've *not* been hired because we were: too creative; not creative enough; too marketing-driven; not marketing-oriented; too big; too small; too aggressive; too laid back; and, my favorite and all-time best reason, 'We just didn't like you guys.' Which of course, seems to me to be the real reason most agency-client relationships turn sour."

PART TWO

The Advertising Agency: Core Departments

3

Account Services

The account executive is the client's representative at the agency. It might be helpful to visualize the account-services department as the hub around which each department within the agency performs its distinct task. The account executive is responsible both for coordinating all of the work performed by the various agency departments and for exacting the best possible work from each for the client he represents. He also makes sure that the account is profitable for the agency and that the client approves all work and costs.

This is a high-pressure job. The account executive has as much at stake as the client in the client's performance in the marketplace. He must understand business, decision making, and marketing. He should know how new products are developed, understanding the technology behind them as well. Good account people enjoy selling and are able to build enthusiasm within the agency for the client and the product.

But they must also present the agency's work to the client. Last, but certainly not least, account representatives must have real "people" skills, able to motivate and manage diverse groups with sometimes conflicting interests.

Together with the client, the account executive identifies marketing problems and plans ways in which the client can build the business. The account executive works with client and agency research departments to obtain information about the marketplace in general and, specifically, about how consumers view the client's product or service. Account services frequently work with research to test new advertising for effectiveness. Account executives work with creatives to develop advertising that is responsive to the client's specific marketing needs. With the media department, account executives make sure that the client's advertising dollars are spent well. In conjunction with the other agency departments, the account executive is responsible for insuring that quality work is done on time and within the prescribed budget.

EVOLUTION

In large agencies, the account-services department is structured to parallel the traditional corporate model, of which Procter & Gamble is the prototype. Originally a candle and soap manufacturer, P & G is today the nation's largest advertiser, spending over $1 billion each year, with over a dozen American advertising agencies handling its many products. P & G used to do its own advertising, creating in 1882 the Ivory Soap tag line still used more than a century later, "99 and $^{44}/_{100}$ percent pure."

As its business expanded to the point where today P & G

has over sixty separate product lines, the company developed a hierarchical structure consisting of assistant brand/product manager, brand/product manager, group brand/product manager, advertising director, and marketing director. In advertising agencies, each department is similarly structured, and each level works with its corporate counterpart on day-to-day business. In account services, the structure consists of assistant account executive, account executive, account supervisor, and management supervisor; in large agencies, success and longevity are often rewarded by vice-presidential titles.

Account people often join advertising agencies after careers on the client side. Says one account executive, "P and G was the training ground for just about everyone in the fifties. Agencies still believe that P and G training, with its emphasis on discipline and well-supported and well-thought-out points of view, is important for account people."

Prior to the 1970s, the account-services departments of most large agencies were almost entirely restricted to white, Protestant men. There were a few Jewish agencies, notably Grey Advertising, which began as an agency specializing in retail clothing accounts. But the emphasis was on staffing account services with those who were the social/religious/educational/gender counterparts of their clients. The primary function of the account person, although usually unstated, was to hold the account and keep the client happy.

Chuck Overholser, recently retired as head of research at Kenyon & Eckhardt (since its recent merger, Bozell, Jacobs, Kenyon & Eckhardt), says: "Part of the old 1950s cliché about account executives was not inaccurate. Account people had good manners, played golf, entertained the client and his wife, and were very good at following up on details and making sure that everything got done. They were good salesmen."

During that period, most agencies had been founded by creatives and still had these founders in the top positions; but, aside from these owner/creatives, clients rarely had contact with anyone in an agency outside account services. The account team presented all creative work, media plans, and research recommendations. In many ways, the account person served as a highly paid messenger, shuttling between client and agency and coordinating work within the agency for the client.

Although it often appeared that account people did little but wine and dine the client, the stress was enormous. If the agency lost an account or a client was unhappy, the account person on that particular piece of business bore the responsibility and was inevitably the first fired by the agency. This is still often true and those in the account-services department occupy the hottest seats in an agency.

During the seventies, however, the account position was significantly professionalized. Most new account people were marketing MBAs who had degrees from the nation's top business schools. They spoke the client's language and understood pricing, distribution, and packaging. These new account managers perceived themselves as sophisticated marketers whose primary job was to build their client's business and direct the strategy of the advertising.

At the same time, most agencies decided that all agency personnel who worked on an account should have client contact and present their own work. Today client responsibility and accountability are shared among the various agency departments with all departments working together to develop, create, and place the advertising for its clients.

36

MAINTAINING THE BUSINESS

Although client accountability is shared, the account person remains the primary agency contact for the client and is the client's advocate within the agency, making sure that the client's advertising dollars are well spent.

This is not an easy position. On the one hand, many account people view themselves as marketing partners with their clients. Account and client together create the marketing plan that explains the rationale for marketing decisions and describes the steps that will be taken to market the product or service. Advertising is only one part of the plan, although in many cases the most important as well as the most expensive. Account people understand the client's long-range objectives and special concerns. In an agency with many clients, the account person pushes to get maximum agency attention and resources for the client he represents.

On the other hand, account people must help clients understand the advertising process and must often defend the work of other departments, particularly creative, to a sometimes overcautious and nervous client. In addition to understanding the client's business, account people must understand creative thinking.

The relationship between account people and creatives can become strained. Creatives sometimes feel that account people are concerned about pleasing the client at the expense of innovative and creative advertising—a "client on the premises," as such account people are referred to. On the other side of the coin, account people sometimes feel that they are perceived simply as client lackeys and that creatives are more concerned about developing ads and commercials that will win awards and make for an impressive portfolio rather than sell the client's product.

Addressing this issue, the late Sandy Sulger, before his death an executive vice president of Ogilvy & Mather, said: "I think that the best creative people regard the best account people as effective and meaningful partners. But they would also regard the best account people as the lesser of this needed combination. Given everything, creatives provide the bridge. We help with the bricks and the steel and tell them where to lay it. But they are the architects and the builders, and that is ultimately the most important."

The best account executives genuinely enjoy working with creatives and count the informal style that the creative department brings to an agency as one of the big pluses of agency work. And the best advertising is created when there is a positive relationship between account and creative, neither one feeling thwarted or intimidated by the other. Jeff Lehman, senior vice president at Advertising to Women, says of this: "A lot of my work involves focusing creatives on what is the most important thing they should be working on at any point of time, motivating them, and helping them overcome discouragement. It can be devastating for a creative to take an idea to the client over which he's sweated and strained and have it rejected. When that happens, you have to stroke and rekindle motivation. A lot of it is hand-holding and recharging the batteries but it takes a lot of care and feeding to get maximum quality and productivity from creative people.

"Part of my job is to absorb the flack when we are not solving creative problems as quickly as the client wants— and they always want it done right away. We try to help clients understand when we haven't achieved their objective in their time frame and sometimes we have to absorb punches. But a smart client knows that he has to be careful of creative people. Criticism should go to the account people. Smart clients don't abuse the creative people in their agencies."

Descriptions of the work of the account services often seem vague and nebulous. Creative develops ads. Research gathers statistics and interprets them. Media recommends the best outlets in which to place the advertising and purchases the time and space; and support departments perform specific tasks. However, the account-services department doesn't produce a tangible product. David Sagarin, a former technical account supervisor at William Esty, and now a partner in his own agency, says of account work: "You are always self-starting, and there is no job description for the day-to-day work account people do. What you are supposed to do is get things done. Most of what you do is high-paid coordination. You make a lot of decisions and you have a lot of responsibility. That's where you earn the money.

"You are making decisions about what advertising to show your client. Here are two layouts. Which is better? Which should we show the client? Here are three strategic points. Which is the one that will make the difference and on which the advertising should be based? What shall we look for in this research? We have two hours of our client's time. What are the most important issues to bring up with the client? Should I bother the client about this? How much money can I spend?

"I have the stewardship of my client's budget and am responsible for the expenditure of some millions of dollars a year to advertise and promote his product. I am also responsible to the agency for spending its money. While the job description is vague and nebulous, it is high stress because, when you are making so many decisions, sometimes you are going to be wrong."

Account executives are usually involved in the client's entire marketing effort, which is why a business background is so helpful. "Although some clients only want advertising," says one account executive, "a client should want and pick its agency so that it can participate in the development of its business strategies, public relations, and new-product development as well as its marketing strategies." Since collateral marketing is increasingly important to clients, advertising-agency account executives must not only be experts on print, radio, and television but must know about direct response, sweepstakes, promotion, direct mail, and event marketing. Says Jed Bernstein, a management supervisor on the Seagram's account at Ogilvy & Mather, "We must be experts on everything that is part of the client's communications and marketing mix." However, it is advertising that usually represents the greatest cost to the client and on which account executives spend most of their time.

Working with creative and research, the account group prepares the creative strategy, which is usually a single page of copy stating fundamentals about the advertising: to whom it should be directed; the key consumer benefit or promise; the reason why the consumer should believe the benefit; and a general statement about product "personality" and feel.

Jed Bernstein gives an example: "When I worked on the American Express account, one of our tasks was to get people to use the card once they had it. Perhaps research shows that out of one hundred people, fifty use their cards and fifty don't. Whatever we are saying to the other fifty isn't right. It's not motivating them because they aren't using the card. I can make some logical guesses but I can also do it more scientifically by going out into the marketplace, isolating the fifty nonusers, and asking them why they don't use the card. From that, I get material that I can use to write a strategy explaining what we want to do—get more American Express cardholders to use the card—and how to get there. Then the creative group can take it and use it as the basis for their advertising."

EXPANDING THE BUSINESS

One of the ongoing tasks of the account executive is the work with the client on building the client's business. This includes implementing current marketing plans and initiating long-term projects such as new-product development, line extenders (new products that bear an existing brand name, such as a shampoo that develops a new formula for dry hair), and new markets for the client's goods. Clients and agencies are continually monitoring the consumer marketplace, anticipating trends in consumer behavior, and planning products and services that will tie in to these trends. At the larger advertising agencies, account executives do yearly analyses of each competing brand or service, gathering every available fact including sales data, distribution, sales according to geographic location and particular stores, sales shelf location, and packaging. Account-services people, particularly those working on high-technology accounts such as electronic equipment and drugs, are so involved in long-term planning that they sign nondisclosure agreements in which they promise to maintain the client's confidentiality.

"As an account person," says Ann Allen, an account supervisor at J. Walter Thompson, "you must understand how major marketers and manufacturers make decisions, how they analyze a brand and a category, the kind of research they do in order to understand and identify their consumers, and the kind of input and thinking that goes into a decision as to who a target audience should be and what the advertising promise should be. We are full partners with the client in developing and marketing the products. Ideally we should be in on everything that has to do with a product from the beginning: naming, packaging, what the package says, where the product appears in the store, pricing, and merchandising."

For instance, research conducted by Burger King and its agency, J. Walter Thompson, showed that there was a developing market for breakfast sales. Together, Burger King and J. Walter Thompson developed breakfast fare and new advertising to promote it. By 1983, Burger King was testing breakfast foods such as the Croissan'wich, omelets, and pancakes in markets including Hartford and Savannah. When a 1985 study by the National Restaurant Association reported that 31.5 percent of all restaurant breakfast purchases came through fast-food outlets, whereas five years before, fast-food outlets accounted for only 18 percent of restaurant breakfast sales, Burger King was ready. In the spring of 1985, according to *ADWEEK*, Burger King spent $15 million on an eight-week national campaign advertising its breakfast foods, including its new Croissan'wich, which "beat the stuffin' out of Egg McMuffin two to one in consumer taste tests."

In addition to developing campaigns for new products or working with the client on new avenues of expansion into the marketplace, account executives constantly monitor their client's performance. When a product starts to slip, the advertising agency is obviously under pressure to explain the reason for the dwindling performance. Sometimes the advertising strategy is wrong and the advertising is ineffective. But sometimes there is a problem with the basic marketing plan. At that point, the account executive frequently gets involved in repositioning the product.

"Our real mission is to create great advertising for our clients," says Jeff Lehman. "The key is to identify a strong, rational product idea that relates to a consumer need or benefit in a new and better way than anything else that's out there in the marketplace. Then we want to surround that rational idea with provocative, memorable, and highly impactable advertising. We believe that the only way you can really ever sell anything is to change the way people feel. And sometimes you know that the product is terrific, but it starts to decline and obviously needs rejuvenation. Repositioning an old product is the most difficult thing that we do. It requires us to overcome what is and somehow change it. We must rekindle enthusiasm, creating and communicating something entirely new."

Minute Rice is an example of a product that was successfully repositioned. When Minute Rice began to lose market share (the percentage of actual retail purchases within the brand category), its manufacturer, General Foods, and its advertising agency, Grey Advertising, commissioned research to see how consumers felt about the product. According to *Madison Avenue*, previous research had shown that during the 1960s, three-quarters of all Minute Rice users were "exclusive users," meaning that they used only Minute Rice. But by the 1980s, 65 percent of those using Minute Rice were dual users, using both the quick-cooking Minute Rice and regular, long-cooking rice, which explained why total sales were down.

When General Foods and Grey analyzed the research results, they discovered that consumers no longer responded to the promise contained in Minute Rice's advertising line, "Foolproof Minute Rice. Perfect rice every time." Whereas the "exclusive user" chose to use Minute Rice to protect her from culinary failure, the "dual user" used Minute Rice to save time in the kitchen. On this basis, General Foods and

Grey repositioned Minute Rice and created advertising to demonstrate that it "Fits the way you cook today." Sales figures show the repositioning a success.

OTHER RESPONSIBILITIES

Not all the work involves new strategies and campaigns. "Most of the time," says Ann Allen, "is spent on the maintenance of the business. Advertising just doesn't begin or end with the commercial." Account executives spend time on the client's premises, usually at least one day a week. Although meetings and presentations are scheduled, most feel that a lot of important information is gained on an informal basis. "It's important to be there," says Jeff Lehman. "You must walk the halls and get a sense of the politics and energy of the client in order to set proper priorities. It's important to have a real understanding and feel of what is going on at a client."

Account people are responsible for making sure that the advertising created is on strategy. Although this is an area of potential conflict between account and creative, Sandy Sulger observed: "We are the gatherers of information and insight in terms of consumer desires and it is up to creative to develop the most effective bridge from where we are now to where we want to be. As representatives of our clients to the creative people, we are often the nay sayers to creative. But often we find that, although the bridge creative has built is good, it's not taking us where we are supposed to be. It's a bridge to nowhere."

The account executive is also responsible for scheduling, insuring that all advertising is accurate, completed on time, and ends up at the right place at the right time. The agency's traffic department must order the proofs to be sent to print media and get television spots to the station in time to be aired; and the copywriter writes the ad quoting the prices; but if the spot is late or the prices wrong, account is ultimately responsible.

All account people talk about the amount of paperwork involved. Most agencies insist upon "contact reports"—summaries of all communications between an agency person and the client—which range from memos reporting a brief telephone conversation to elaborate records of meetings and presentations. Harold Sogard, an assistant account executive at Ogilvy & Mather, estimates that a quarter of his time is spent writing reports and summarizing meetings. But as Dave Sagarin says, "You are dealing with so much ambiguity all the time, especially if you are in the midst of working on a new ad, and there are literally hundreds of points that arise. You don't want to have disagreement on the next draft. And don't forget, whenever there are substantive issues, people often have a different perception of what happened. So memos are a good idea."

The way in which an account person balances the need to concentrate on seemingly small details while maintaining an overall vision of client and agency needs is what distinguishes a good and effective account person from an indifferent and possibly destructive one. Excess caution and too much attention to detail leads to the kind of account person creatives find so difficult. But good, strong account groups motivate creatives to produce even better and more effective advertising than they might do under other circumstances.

Ted Bates's Jerry Brady says: "The account group often determines how a client is perceived within the agency. The best situation is one in which research, media, and creative all work together and understand the contribution that each makes to the client's business. Too many times, there is too much emphasis on memos, meetings, and administrative details. The best thing is when the account group makes everybody who works on that account within the agency really care about the business and produce for it."

One of the less visible functions of account people is their ability to generate information and communication within the client organization. Although agency structure parallels the client organization and is hierarchical, communications within the agency aren't. Agencies tend to be informal places with people at all levels, regardless of title, talking to one another and to those in other departments. This is not true in most corporations. Speaking to this issue, one account executive commented, "The thing that a strong agency can bring to a client is a degree of independence. Often the client culture, although not on purpose, develops a kind of sameness to the way it does things and the way it looks at things. Everyone reports vertically. We have the ability to argue and the strength and confidence to do it."

Even assistant account executives usually have mobility within an agency, a situation that is very different from the one at their corporate counterparts. Says one beginning account executive: "Here at the agency, if we want information, we go directly to the person who has it. But when the president of our client division wants to be briefed, even though it's someone five levels down who knows what is really happening in that particular area, the person who actually does the briefing is the person right under the president."

It's obvious that an agency account-services representative requires many different, and in some ways, contradictory skills. Account reps are savvy business people who understand the often capricious nature of the marketplace.

They are organizers and coordinators who must also be loose enough to understand creative thinking. They are balancers, able to function in frequently stratified corporate environments while being effective in the often freewheeling atmosphere of the advertising agency. As personalities, account executives are achievement-oriented. They want to see results.

"I think that the agency business is both semiconfrontational and semientrepreneurial," said Sandy Sulger. "You must enjoy the selling process—the act of knowing more, doing it better, improving it, beating the competition. Good account people are competitive and somewhat manipulative. They like to change people's minds on the basis of having better background, intuitive flashes, words, pictures, hard work, disciplined thinking—all the tools. They are disappointed when they fail, and not because clients are yelling or sales are bad. It's just, 'Damnit, I was wrong.'"

JOBS

There is less emphasis on MBA degrees today than even a few years ago, although, according to the September 1985 issue of *Madison Avenue* magazine, certain agencies, such as Young & Rubicam and BBDO, still recruit primarily at top graduate schools, including Harvard, Wharton, Northwestern, UCLA, and Stanford. However, many other agencies, such as Grey, McCann-Erickson, and Ogilvy & Mather no longer require the degree.

This is in part because marketing is no longer as attractive to business-school graduates, finance having supplanted it both in terms of salary and prestige. The most qualified and desirable business-school graduates are not entering advertising as they did during the 1970s, although, as Ann Allen points out, "One of the things that's fun about this business is that you can move fast. You can have a high level of responsibility sooner in advertising than in most other businesses."

College graduates with strong academic backgrounds can enter as assistant account executives with a median starting salary of $18,000 to $23,000. MBAs start at salaries of $26,000 to $34,000. Fran Devereux, senior vice president/personnel director at Ogilvy & Mather, points out that the salary gap has become wider between client and agency. "We don't match what our clients pay," she says, "but we do believe that you will move faster in terms of responsibility and an interesting job and that it will all even out within a few years. But it's a hard sell. Most people have debts and want the money. Also, some MBAs had very high expectations when they came to work for an agency. They wanted to run businesses and when they had to do backroom stuff for a few years, they became bored and unhappy."

A look at some account-services people shows a great diversity in background.

Ann Allen, of J. Walter Thompson, holds an undergraduate degree in English from Harvard and a master's in English literature from the University of Cambridge. Planning to pursue a career in academia, she decided to "be sure in my own mind that I could make it in the real world." She began as a copywriter on a book-club account in a direct-mail agency.

Jeff Lehman, of Advertising to Women, was previously an assistant product manager at Mead Johnson, where he was responsible for marketing PAL'S children's vitamins in animal shapes. When Bristol-Myers purchased Mead Johnson, PAL'S became part of the Bristol-Myers over-the-counter toiletries and drugs division; Lehman was promoted to product manager, then group manager, and finally to marketing director, handling analgesics and deodorants and antiperspirants. "In 1980, I decided to switch. I felt a desire and need to build my career; and, from a professional standpoint, I realized that the work I enjoyed most was the advertising part. Not only that, but I felt that advertising was potentially the most productive part of the business. It is the part of the marketing mix that can make the largest difference."

Ogilvy & Mather's Harold Sogard was a theatrical general manager before making a career change and entering advertising at the age of thirty. "I wanted something that would give me greater intellectual challenge, more financial reward, and an opportunity for more of a personal life than I could have in the theater, as I was on the road so much of the time. I talked to people in various fields, and advertising kept coming up as an area that could use my skills and one that would interest me."

David Sagarin, former technical account supervisor on the Minolta account at William Esty, had been an editor of a group of photographic magazines that he wrote as well as edited.

Jerry Brady, of Ted Bates, is a Harvard Business School graduate who concentrated on finance but discovered that he liked marketing more. "It became clear to me that when you are marketing parity products with parity packaging, parity pricing, and parity channels of distribution, it is advertising that creates a perceived difference among purchasers. It isn't apparent why one product is any better than the other just by looking at it. Advertising is what makes the difference. I also decided that I would rather work with people who were writers, art directors, and producers rather than people who were on the manufacturing side."

Most of the larger agencies have account-management training programs for assistant account executives. Usually consisting of lunchtime seminars conducted over a period of six months, the programs acquaint beginners with the way agencies work and what the various agency departments do. Most include a project in which trainees from various departments get together and develop a simulated advertising plan, including research and media objectives. Among those agencies with specific account training programs are N W Ayer, BBDO, Ted Bates Advertising, Benton & Bowles, Campbell-Ewald, Doyle Dane Bernbach, Foote, Cone & Belding, McCann-Erickson, SSC & B, J. Walter Thompson, and Young & Rubicam.

4

Research

Crayola crayons! Every child uses them and most adults automatically reach for the green-and-yellow box when purchasing crayons. An easy sell, one would think. Just make sure they're in the stores and in toy and school-equipment catalogues. However, in 1983, Binney & Smith, manufacturers of Crayola, had a new president, Richard S. Gurin, who took over after a twenty-three-year career at Procter & Gamble. Crayola hadn't advertised for a year and Gurin's mandate was to increase sales and build the business by tapping the largest market possible for the product. Before directing Crayola's agency, Needham, Harper Worldwide, to come up with new advertising material, Gurin decided to find out some facts about the product and its consumers.

Together, agency and client commissioned research to find out who purchased the crayons and how they were used. They discovered that most crayons are purchased by mothers between the ages of twenty-five and forty-nine. Practically all of these crayons are purchased for children between the ages of two and seven. About 60 percent of these children use crayons more than once a day, and practically all use crayons at least once a day. An average of two to seven crayons are used daily. Researchers also discovered that these Crayola-using families purchased the crayons two to three times a year.

Based upon these results, Crayola and Needham, Harper knew who was using the product and how it was being used. They identified their target audience, the group to which the advertising must be directed. They knew when people purchased the crayons so they could plan optimum times in which to run advertising. Finally, agency and client confirmed that the advertising goal was not so much to get people to use Crayons but to persuade them to purchase them more frequently.

Once Crayola and Needham, Harper compiled the basic consumer and product information, they commissioned additional research to discover the message that would motivate that target audience to purchase more crayons. Asking respondents to rank a list of attributes they considered most important when purchasing play materials for their children, researchers discovered that mothers cared most about their children's feelings of accomplishment. With this information, Needham, Harper could now develop a strategy on which to base advertising.

Creative material was developed on the basis of what was called a "loop." Mother purchases crayons and gives them to her child. The child then draws and gives the drawing as a gift to Mother. To Needham, Harper, this loop represented a tangible way to show a child's sense of accomplishment. Whereas Crayola's earlier advertising had used the tag line,

"It's fun to create with Crayola!"—a line targeted more at children—out of this new strategy came a new tag line, "Crayola draws you closer," implicitly acknowledging that it is the mother, as purchaser, to whom the advertising must be directed.

Needham, Harper developed its Crayola media plan on the basis of the research results as well. Called the Crayola Holiday Network, television time was purchased on network and syndicated specials broadcast at holiday time. Media planners specifically selected family television specials—shows that tend to be viewed by parents and children together. Actual numbers are confidential; but, according to Needham, Harper account supervisor Susan Spohn, the first year of the new Crayola campaign, 1985, was an outstanding year.

Advertisers use research both to gather facts about consumers and the marketplace so that creative strategy can be developed and to test creative material to see whether it accomplishes the strategic goals. In agencies with research departments, researchers work with clients and the account group to build and expand the client's business. But even small agencies without in-house research departments conduct research studies for their clients, retaining independent research suppliers.

Clifford Emery says: "We were retained by a bank in a small New England town. They wanted to be visible and announce themselves to the community. We believed that in order to establish a direction for itself, the bank would have to know how people perceived it. We commissioned a research study to give us some information upon which we could more effectively base our advertising and marketing.

"For instance, do older people think differently about the bank than those who are younger? Are there differences by sex or income level? Maybe we would discover that middle-income people like the bank but not those with high income, which is the group we would want to attract for trust services. If someone asked you to recommend that bank, to whom would you recommend it and why? How would you rank it for various categories such as knowledgeable people, innovative services, or convenient hours?

"When we looked at the results, we discovered that the bank was well thought of, but people didn't perceive it to be different from any other bank in the area. So we decided to give the bank a special identity and created advertising to highlight its community involvement. Formerly, the bank's advertising was pretty much like any other bank's. It looked formal and talked only about the services it provided. Now the ads use a script type that helps project warmth, and emphasizes community as well as banking services. We plan to run this advertising for about a year and then run new research in order to see whether the bank's image has changed."

Research departments in agencies today are much smaller than they were even a decade ago. This doesn't mean that research is less important. It is just a reflection of the changes in the way research operates. Whereas agencies used to conduct their own research studies and projects, today most of the actual hands-on research is carried out by research suppliers. This is a growing business. According to *Advertising Age*, the top forty U.S. marketing/advertising/public-opinion research companies and the fifty-four survey-research companies that are members of the Council of American Survey Research Organizations showed gross worldwide revenues of $1.56 billion in 1984. In addition, most client organizations today have their own research departments and certainly don't want to pay their agencies for duplicate work.

Some people actually feel it advantageous to work with agencies that don't have their own in-house research departments. Dickison & Radaseder's Don Dickison says: "We prefer not to have staff research people. The big problem with an agency having its own research department is credibility. Often an agency has a pet campaign it wants to get through and if their research people do the study, it might be weighted, however unconsciously. A client usually feels better with an outside research firm. It's like a third neutral party."

Agencies and clients commission custom research from suppliers, working with them on the research design and data analysis but relying on the supplier for the fieldwork and data gathering. They also purchase syndicated research from suppliers. Simmons Market Research Bureau, for instance, offers its subscribers access to a data base created from a comprehensive survey of 19,000 adults. This body of information includes data on the purchase and use of products and services in eight hundred categories, which include 3,900 brands; the media these people use; and their demographics and life-style orientation.

The position of agency research departments varies from agency to agency. *Advertising Age* reported that an Advertising Research Foundation survey found that 87 percent of agency creative directors believed that research was important in creating advertising and yet only 47 percent said that research was always provided when they were developing campaigns. Forty-two percent said that they didn't even know the names of the research people working on their accounts; and 34 percent perceived themselves as "totally isolated from the research department."

Chuck Overholser says: "Agencies differ a great deal in regard to what senior management thinks about research and planning. Some chief executives insist that it be done and others not at all. Research is thought of as a peripheral service for the client's own marketing department and also as providing a certain specific type of information for the agency. Often, researchers are not seen as key members of the team."

Although there is great diversity in agency research departments, the trend is for researchers to take on an increasingly active role in long-range business planning for their clients. Agency researchers work with the client determining client research needs and then work with an independent supplier who performs the actual data gathering. Beginning researchers spend time learning the technical skills involved in research, including coding, editing, and tabulating information, but agency researchers are increasingly specialists, advising clients and the account-services departments as to what research is needed and then analyzing the implications of the results. Agency researchers are today apt to refer to themselves as strategic planners instead of researchers. They work with clients on expanding the client's business, developing new markets for products, and new products to fill niches in the marketplace.

In some agencies, researchers develop ten-year plans, forecasting changes in the marketplace and identifying new products that may result from new technology or developing social trends. One researcher says: "You try to identify what places to go in the future. For instance, technology has made possible the introduction of a lot of new products recently, including VCRs, compact discs, and home health testing kits. We try to forecast future opportunities for our clients."

Edith Gilson, head of the Consumer Behavior Group at J. Walter Thompson, says: "Talking to the same user over and over might sell product but it won't make the business grow. To accomplish that, there are choices. I can take business away from the competition. I can increase the frequency of use among the present users; or I can increase the category in which my client's product or service is placed by bringing new users in. That's how Seven-Up, the 'Uncola,' was developed. Seven-Up was primarily used as a mixer. It couldn't grow as a mixer so we positioned it in the soft-drink category. Today decaffeinated soft drinks are a category in themselves."

Where researchers are held in high esteem, they are integral members of the team working on the client's business. Edith Gilson says: "Account and research are almost interchangeable. We are the representatives of the consumer. The account people represent the client, the product, and the business. As a researcher, given what I know about the consumers and the nature of the product, I can tell what will work and what won't work. I work with creative people so they have the necessary information on which to base executions."

To bring researchers into strategic planning for clients, some agencies have established a new position called account planning. Modeled on a system currently used in most British advertising agencies, the concept of account planning is not new. It was initiated by J. Walter Thompson's office in Great Britain during the 1960s, although a similar system had developed at Young & Rubicam during the 1950s.

The traditional agency researcher gathers information and interprets it to the account representative, who then works with creative in forming the advertising strategy. But under the account-planning system, a planner works directly with the team to create the strategy, playing the role of the consumer during strategy sessions. Instead of merely giving a statistic or number and explaining its possible implications, the planner portrays the meaning of the figures in terms of human behavior or emotion and what impact it will have in the marketplace.

Chuck Overholser comments: "There are good and bad things about the account-planning function. The good side is that to a considerable degree planners understand consumer behavior and attitudes and are able to influence the creative product in that direction. On the bad side is that at its worst the planner can become the rationalizer and salesman for the creative director."

Overholser, who was at Young & Rubicam in the fifties, remembers a two-tier research system. In it, most agency researchers worked as conventional researchers, carrying out research projects and studies. In addition, a new position, that of agency research account executive, was created to analyze and interpret the results in the context of the consumer and the marketplace. At the time, the idea caught on not in the United States but in Great Britain. J. Walter Thompson's Edith Gilson says: "The researchers in Great Britain were all scientists and not as practical as American researchers are today. The account people were called *contactors*, and they established the contact between agency and client. And that was it. There was a void, with no one developing client business, initiating strategies, or doing long-term planning. British agencies decided to take some of the more practical, strategic-oriented researchers and put them into an account-planner group. The more technically oriented people remained as researchers and analysts. The account planner does exactly what the term implies: His main concern is planning and not the client relationship. He is a thinker, marketer, and analyzer."

In advertising, research is used in several areas. *Market research* investigates the public as the consumer. It examines how the public thinks, what it wants, and why it acts the way it does. *Concept testing* assesses consumer reaction to a product or to the way a product is presented through its advertising. *Copy testing* determines whether the advertising is effective and is accomplishing its goals.

MARKET RESEARCH

Advertisers need to obtain basic information about the marketplace before they can even begin to create ads. This is market research. Edith Gilson says: "Good commercials come from good strategy; and the strategy comes from a thorough understanding of three elements: the client's business, the consumer, and the product environment."

When developing creative strategy, the client and agency decide to whom the advertising message should be directed and the best way to communicate it. But in order to do that, advertisers must first know how consumers feel about the client's product or service, its competition, and general trends in the marketplace.

"Research," says Chuck Overholser, "is an attempt to narrow the options. Research helps us to identify the market target, the competition to our client's particular product or service, the benefits consumers seek, circumstances in which consumers use the product, reasons why they don't use the product or service, any competitive leverage that the brand or service may have against others, and how the brand or service is perceived. All of this is the basis on which advertising strategies can be developed."

In performing market research, researchers employ various research techniques.

Demographic research enables researchers to isolate consumers according to specific characteristics such as age, income, occupation, educational level, and race, as well as family characteristics such as number of children or whether individuals are married, single, or divorced.

For example, *American Demographics* published a study in 1984 that described a category called "empty nesters," which was composed of 22.2 million people ranging in age from fifty-five to sixty-four. People in this category travel frequently, are 50 percent more likely to own a second home than people ten years younger, buy and sell more stocks, and purchase more garden supplies and materials than any other age group. This kind of study identifies potential consumers for an advertiser's products and services and suggests ways in which business may expand into new areas. It also helps select the target audiences toward whom creative can direct the advertising message.

Psychographic research analyzes consumer behavior, attitude, and emotional responses. For instance, studies of teenage girls show that they have a fragile sense of self-identity and are not sure of themselves as individuals. In the marketplace, this is reflected by fads and an almost total lack of long-term brand loyalty. Research by Helene Curtis Industries, reported in the *Wall Street Journal*, shows that the average teenage girl tries four different brands of shampoo each year whereas older women try 1.5.

One of the most popular and widely known psychographic research programs originated and is administered by the Stanford Research Institute. Its Values and Lifestyles program (VALS) provides prototype consumer profiles to subscribing agencies and businesses.

Based on consumer responses to questions designed to elicit attitudes about politics, work, products, education, life-style and self-image, VALS has defined nine life-style types that are then grouped into four categories. These categories include "Need-Driven," which is composed of "Survivors" and "Sustainers"; the "Inner-Directed," in which are placed the "I-am-Me's," "Experientials," and the "Societally Conscious"; the "Outer-Directed," which consists of the "Belongers," "Emulators," and "Achievers"; and the "Integrated."

Advertisers can use these consumer-group characteristics to develop strategy and create ads that are specifically directed toward these carefully identified consumer groups. For example, the "Survivors" and "Sustainers," which make up the "Need-Driven" group, are those with little disposable income and whose buying decisions are based upon need. Those within the "Inner-Directed" category are consumers whose purchasing decisions are based upon personal wants and social responsibility rather than outside expectations.

VALS projects trends as well. Although the Outer-Directed category comprises more than 50 percent of the population, Inner-Directeds are becoming the most influential and fastest-growing segment in the nation. According to the trade journal *Marketing and Media Decisions*, it is estimated that the Inner-Directeds will make up 60 percent of the population by 1990. And advertisers are responding to this trend.

For example, according to VALS theory, a mother in the Inner-Directed category is not going to respond to a message like "You, you're the one" and take her brood to McDonald's for hamburgers when she "deserves a break today" and doesn't feel like cooking. That pitch appeals to an Outer-Directed mother. An Inner-Directed mother, however, tends to be health-conscious and might take the kids to McDonald's if there a salad bar. Burger King and

Wendy's, no slouches themselves when it comes to research, know that the Inner-Directed is more likely to respond to ads that say: "You'll never have to eat a *fried* quarter pounder again" or "100 percent *natural* boneless breast of chicken."

When researchers undertake market research, they do quantitative and qualitative studies. *Quantitative* research looks at actual numbers. For instance, a researcher might simply tabulate yes/no or like/dislike responses on a questionnaire. The information gathered should be projectable to the national population.

Qualitative research explores differences in feeling and condition and is often used to develop hypotheses that can then be tested quantitatively. It gives advertisers insights into consumer emotions and beliefs. It is more expensive than quantitative research because researchers conduct lengthy interviews with respondents and spend more time analyzing results. Qualitative research projects are frequently followed up by a quantitative study in order to make sure that the qualitative results are projectable and real.

Computers have taken over a lot of the "number-crunching" work that researchers used to do. More and more researchers are able to use their time analyzing what the numbers and statistics mean instead of compiling and organizing figures. This has meant that researchers must be careful to remember that their analysis and conclusions must be based upon carefully executed studies.

Edith Gilson says: "In research, we use scientific method, but research is not scientific. Writing a questionnaire and analyzing data are creative. When I write a questionnaire, I am trying to have a dialogue with another person. I must be extremely careful about how I phrase questions because how I ask the question will often determine the response I get.

The same goes with analyzing the numbers. You must be careful as a researcher. Very often, when we design a study we have gut feeling and a hypothesis, but you must leave yourself open for the challenge."

When advertisers commission research studies from outside suppliers, it is the task of the research department to interpret the vast quantity of material that results. As one advertising researcher says: "Numbers sit dead on a page and the perspective of the supplier who does the study is to look at every number in every single way possible and write a huge report. The supplier isn't very market-oriented and often doesn't even know the purpose or concept behind the study. We must interpret the numbers in a way that not only makes sense and can be supported but can be acted upon in making decisions within the agency and client organization."

CONCEPT TESTING

Concept testing, or creative research, as it is often called, tests strategy to see if it is effective. For instance, an agency launching a new breakfast cereal will consider several possible advertising strategies. One might emphasize convenience, another the cereal's ingredients, and still another its great taste. Agencies and clients frequently decide to do concept tests in order to ascertain which strategy elicits a positive response from the desired consumer group. Consumers are shown concepts in one of a variety of forms, including brief statements about a new product or a visual with a block of copy.

Advertisers often use focus groups during the concept-testing stage. In focus groups, several or more consumers are paid a small sum of money to talk informally about their feelings or reactions to products or concepts. Trained moderators show participants new product ideas and advertising concepts and the group then discusses its reactions and feelings.

There are over seven hundred facilities throughout the nation that hold focus groups several times a week, charging clients about two thousand to three thousand dollars a group. Most research suppliers and agencies use the services of professional focus-group recruiters who try to insure that the groups consist of potential consumers of the product or service being tested and that participants fit demographic criteria, such as age and sex, for the target audience.

While focus groups can be helpful, it is important that advertisers understand their limitations. Chuck Overholser points out that most researchers state that focus groups are used in order to give advertisers a general feeling about consumer reaction to the product or advertising sample. But too often, he says, researchers interpret focus-group results as if they were real research results, which they are not. "There is no degree of accuracy with them. But there are certain things you can get from focus groups, such as insights, that you don't get from rigorously standard controlled experiments. These are subtleties, turns of phrase, complex responses and reactions that might go unnoticed in a standard experimental design. Also it's really good for creatives to listen to consumers talk about a product. Usually the creative person's social network is atypical of the market and if you can get creatives to someplace like Kansas or somewhere outside of their usual milieu, they are likely to get some ideas that they might not otherwise have gotten."

Creatives are the ones who find focus groups most valuable at this stage of the advertising process. Jack Sidebotham, co-creative director at McCaffrey and McCall, says:

"Most people need direction. I recently had some ideas that I thought were terrific but when they were shown before six different focus groups, the groups indicated that the things I thought were wonderful were terrible. All of us appreciate that kind of guidance. There is no point in creating a monument to yourself. A beautiful piece of art that doesn't communicate what you want and need is a waste."

COPY TESTING

Copy testing tests advertising material for effectiveness. Television is the advertising most frequently tested in advance, primarily because production and television time are so expensive that advertisers don't want to take risks. Although a television spot is ideally tested in finished form, advertisers usually choose not to spend the thousands of dollars it costs to produce one, opting instead to test the spot in one of the following forms: *Animatics* are artwork, either cartoons or drawings, that show limited movement. *Photomatics* are photographs shot in sequence on film. *Liveamatics* show live talent filmed against simple props simulating the commercial content. *Ripamatics* recombine footage from various other spots. Frequently a taped soundtrack is used as background.

Technology has made possible a whole gamut of testing techniques. VOPAN, voice pitch analysis, measures the rate at which the vocal cords vibrate while consumers talk about their reactions to advertisements they are shown. The faster the vibrations, the more involved the consumer is. There are eye-tracking techniques in which respondents look at advertising under laboratory conditions, and the exact spot on which the eye focuses is determined. Galvanic skin response measures the power of a message to excite or arouse the subject; and brain-wave interpretation can measure whether or not a consumer is taking in a message even though he may be unaware of it. Unfortunately, not only are these techniques expensive but researchers are not really sure how to interpret their meanings.

Advertisers can test to see if the spot motivates consumers to go out and buy the product or use the service. Consumers are taken into a theater to view actual television programs and commercials. They are then questioned about the programs and commercials and their responses are analyzed. Other techniques include shopping-mall intercepts in which shoppers are invited to visit a testing center and are asked to give their opinions about advertising shown to them.

Advertisers can also take a finished spot and air it in a few cities as a test, using what is called "day-after recall." The day after the commercial is aired, a sample of people are called to see if they remember viewing the commercial and if so to tell the caller the name of the product.

There is a certain amount of controversy about copy testing in general, particularly day-after recall. Copywriters sometimes say, "I'm writing for Burke," meaning Burke Marketing Services, the research company that does most pre- and post-TV copy testing. One writer says: "If your material doesn't score well on Burke, you're back to square one. Unfortunately, with Burke it's a one-time thing. People see the spot once and if they remember it, great. If not, forget it. Some advertising has to grow on you before you really hear what is being said. It takes more than one viewing for the impact to hit. We often end up writing some kind of banger opening in front—a door slamming, a big chord of music— something up front that will jar the ear so the viewer will perk up and listen. You may lose your audience halfway through, but a lot of clients are living by these scores and you must keep that in mind when you are writing."

Packaged goods, which tend to be parity products, have the highest advertising-to-sales ratio (the ratio of advertising dollars spent on a product to actual sales). In a parity product, it is the advertising that creates the good's identity and that is the primary marketing tool. Therefore, packaged-goods advertisers are less willing to take risks in advertising, frequently opting for safety and relying on test results.

Ron Berger, of Messner, Vetere, Berger, Carey, formerly with Ally & Gargano/MCA Advertising, says: "Companies like MCI and Federal Express test their commercials but they do it the right way. They aren't ruled by it. They've gotten winners out of commercials that tested badly, and vice versa. To dismiss everything that doesn't test well means that your opinion is meaningless. Too many people allow the numbers to make decisions for them."

There is also controversy about whether using anything other than a finished commercial can give accurate results. Edith Gilson says: "I am completely against pretesting creative in animatic form. Most copy-testing techniques do not have the flexibility, and it depends upon who you ask as to the answers you get. When we recommend pretesting, the material must be in final form and the research custom-designed. It's expensive, but why do something that misleads you?"

There is a consensus, however, that focus groups are not the place to test creative product. Jack Sidebotham says: "Focus groups can be destructive if they are allowed to become ad hoc creative directors passing judgment on finished ads. It is one thing to get opinions about concepts but another to get criticism about type, style, and layout."

On the same theme, Chuck Overholser says: "There are

two ways that focus groups are badly misused. One is to kill things and the other is to sell things. There is a great temptation on the part of agencies to use focus groups as part of the selling process to the client, to say, 'We showed it to three focus groups and they loved it.' But if you do that, then the client expects to be part of the process.

"We keep talking about partnership with our clients but we really don't want partnership during the creative process, and there shouldn't be. Agencies should tell the client that focus groups provide valuable information but that the information gathered will never be used to support the agency's advertising recommendations."

TEST MARKETING

One of the best ways to test advertising (and new products) is to try it out in a test market. Certain cities are targeted as good places in which to test products and the advertising that will be used to sell them.

New technology gives researchers the ability to gather information with an accuracy and depth impossible just a few years ago. Services such as BehaviorScan, operated by Information Resources Inc., monitor buying patterns and television viewing habits of its member households in eight minimarkets. These test cities are chosen with exacting criteria. The population must be between 100,000 and 150,000 and the nearest shopping district fifty or more miles away. The test city must have at least ten supermarkets that can be equipped with specially installed scanners, and there must be a local newspaper that can run ads and coupons. At least 75 percent of the population must have cable television.

Whenever a BehaviorScan family shops at a grocery or a

drugstore, its purchases are recorded by the scanners. Microcomputers attached to the television set monitor what the family watches. Through cable TV, special ads are shown to see whether or not they affect buying patterns.

Needless to say, test marketing is very expensive and is usually done by only the largest clients. For instance, Procter & Gamble test marketed Solo laundry detergent in Erie, Pennsylvania; Omaha; Buffalo and Rochester, New York; in Maine; and in parts of Vermont and New Hampshire. Budweiser Light Beer was test marketed in Charlotte, North Carolina; Little Rock, Arkansas; Omaha; Pensacola, Florida; San Antonio; and Tucson, Arizona.

One of the oldest test-market cities is Columbus, Ohio. Its test-market history began in 1944 when the square milk bottle was introduced there. Since then, Columbus has been one of the test markets for such products as family-size Coke, Nescafé Instant Coffee, Comet, disposable diapers, computerized banking, and Stouffer's Lean Cuisine frozen entrées. Advertisers look for certain criteria when selecting cities to be test markets. The city must be large enough to represent a significant purchasing activity but small enough to be monitored easily by researchers. Demographically the city must represent the consumers marketers are trying to reach—which, with package goods, tend to be young, upscale but middle-class professionals. It must have a stable economy, so that people actually have disposable income.

In addition to having its own newspapers, television, and radio stations, a test city should be geographically isolated from other urban areas and not have easy access to other media. When clients test new products, they want to control the product messages and information disseminated to the consumer so that research results will be as accurate as possible.

When all is said and done, even the most sophisticated marketers can make mistakes. The basic research design may be faulty or results can be badly interpreted or analyzed. In April 1985, Coca-Cola announced that it was reformulating its drink. The company had spent two years and over $4 million on research that showed that most of the over 190,000 consumers who participated in taste tests preferred the sweeter, less fizzy taste of the new Coke. According to the *New York Times*, an estimated $10 million advertising campaign was planned to support the new product.

To celebrate, Coke also introduced the reformulated drink to over six thousand guests at New York's Radio City Music Hall in a ceremony that included Ray Charles, the Harlem Boys Choir, the American Symphony Orchestra, and the Rockettes. Guests were shown new advertising created by McCann-Erickson, including national television commercials, local television commercials, radio spots, Hispanic, black, and special advertising for strong Coke markets, for strong Pepsi markets, and for parity markets in which Coke and Pepsi were equal. There was a special commercial for use during the period after the announcement of the reformulation but before the new Coke was actually available in stores. For the time when new Coke became available, there were commercials featuring the "Coke is it" jingle.

But the company didn't count on people's reactions to the withdrawal of old Coke. A ground swell of protest arose. Old Coke diehards organized an Old Coca-Cola Drinkers of America protest group and a letter-writing campaign. Finally, on July 11, the Coca-Cola Company announced that it was reviving old Coca-Cola under the name "Coke Classic." Both old and new Coke would be available.

Research had never examined how people would feel about having old Coke taken away from them. In its concern for secrecy about the reformulation, Coca-Cola and its research supplier never told the consumers who participated in taste tests that old Coke was going to be abandoned.

Most researchers believe that advertising research should aid in making judgments but should never take the place of common sense. Even with careful methodology and strict controls, research techniques are not exact. Rather, research provides direction and a point of departure for advertisers to use in creating effective advertising. As Edith Gilson says: "Research can weed out disaster. But research doesn't distinguish between excellent and very good. And excellent is what we need and what we want."

JOBS

Agency research departments parallel the tiered structure of other departments within the agency, with groups consisting of beginning research trainees, junior project directors, assistant research executives or market research analysts, and those in positions of seniority, including project directors, research account executives, associate research directors, and, at the head, research directors. All the groups work under a department head. In some agencies, groups handle all the research business for specific accounts and in others groups work on a per-project basis.

Whereas research used to be seen as a stepping-stone to something else, usually a career in marketing, research is increasingly a career of choice. Some agencies hire beginning researchers just out of college but most hire researchers who have had prior experience working for research suppliers or who hold graduate degrees. Entry-level salaries vary from $13,500 to $23,000, depending upon education and experience.

Increasingly, computer literacy is assumed for entering

researchers. Most agencies don't require researchers to hold advanced degrees in statistics or mathematics, although a basic knowledge of research technique is desired. Agencies hire research personnel from all disciplines, including English, psychology, sociology, anthropology, and the other social sciences.

Describing the hiring process, Chuck Overholser says, "The kind of people I look for have some formal training in experimental design and statistic methodology but basically I look for people who I believe can think straight, write well, talk articulately, get along with people, and who I believe have a certain amount of potential to make mature judgments under often difficult situations."

In the larger agencies that tend to deal with large corporate clients, both client and agency usually have a research staff. And, as is true in account services, agency research people often find that although the departmental model parallels the client model, communications within the agency are much less formal than within the client organization. This, says Overholser, gives advertising researchers a "lot more clout and power than their marketing counterparts. They have more input in the agency and also have access to the brand managers at the client. They must therefore be good people operators, able to get along with the client side and of course those at the agency."

If the client doesn't have a research department, agencies often initiate and suggest research projects for the client. If the client does have a research department, the agency often gets research information from the client—although this isn't always easy. As one researcher says: "There is often a certain amount of overlap in our research and the client's and often we are asked to take work done by the client and use it. As consumers of the client's work, we check its accuracy and make sure that the information is useful. Clients may be reluctant to share confidential information with us, especially in the beginning of the relationship. They'll give us a report but not the basic results—which is what we need. We want to mine all the information to see if anything has been missed.

"As advertising researchers, we often have different analytic skills. Corporate researchers are more oriented toward the business needs of the client and concentrate on data that is product-related and predictive of consumer fit with the product. We are more concerned with consumer need and product-imagery needs. Most people think that the account representative handles all the client communication. But we are constantly meeting face to face with our research counterparts. Developing good relationships with them is a very important part of our work."

5

Creative

The creative department is where the actual advertising is conceived and developed. When people think of the advertising business, creative is usually what comes to mind. Advertising's reputation as a glamour business emanates from this department. Popular fantasy portrays an art director or copywriter accompanied by a photographer, models in tow, running from one exotic location to another.

Reality is, of course, quite different. The location is more than likely to be a photography studio located in an area in which rents are low enough to allow the photographer to afford the kind of space he needs. The model, an actor portraying a man with a bad head cold, is grateful to be working and constantly checks his watch so that he won't be late for his next audition. The art director, concerned that the backdrop against which the cold remedy is featured clashes with the package color, is frantically searching through pieces of material. And the copywriter is exhausted from having written over a dozen different pieces of advertising copy before finally getting a go-ahead from the client.

It is true that advertising creatives tend to be more casually dressed than others in the agency. Mary Wells Lawrence, founder and chairman of Wells, Rich, Greene, is said to have once sent a memo requesting that women refrain from wearing jeans on the day an important potential client was expected. In contrast to that of account services, media, and research, the ambience in the creative department is informal, with individual office decor reflecting more of the occupant's personality. But art directors and copywriters are not artistic prima donnas. They are professionals, working for a profit-making business whose job is to sell the products and services of its clients.

Today's creative department has its genesis in the 1960s, the period often referred to as the "creative revolution." This was not only a time in which some classy and witty advertising appeared—in contrast to the hard-selling seriousness of the 1950s—but a time in which the status of creatives, particularly art directors, was elevated.

If any agency can be said to have inspired this "revolution," it was Doyle Dane Bernbach, founded in 1949 with a capital investment of only $1,200. According to the "Agency Profiles" issue of *Advertising Age*, Doyle Dane Bernbach had almost $1.6 billion in worldwide billings in 1985. At the time of its merger with BBDO and Needham Harper, it was the world's seventh largest agency. Under the creative direction of William Bernbach, the agency garnered a reputation for creating inspired campaigns and ads that combined elegance, humor, outstanding writing and artwork, and respect for the consumer.

When he founded Doyle Dane Bernbach, Mr. Bernbach

implemented what was then an innovative structure: He paired copywriters and art directors into teams that worked together to create advertising. For creatives, Doyle Dane was a wonderful place to work. Saatchi & Saatchi senior vice president David Herzbrun, a Doyle Dane Bernbach alumnus, says, "Everybody worth a damn in the business was here. It was a terrific atmosphere, with very little backbiting or competition. Everybody was excited about everybody else's work. We were trying to prove some things—Jewish and Italian isn't bad, intelligence and wit are okay, and the public isn't stupid."

Many of the ads created at Doyle Dane Bernbach are classics, still remembered over a quarter of a century later. "You don't have to be Jewish to love Levy's real Jewish rye" featured photographs of non-Jewish ethnics with Levy's rye. These ads made Levy's the largest-selling rye bread in New York. The "We try harder" campaign for Avis made that car-rental business's second-place status a plus, portraying it as an eager and attractive underdog when compared to complacent, uncaring, number-one Hertz. And in the big-car decade of the fifties in which chrome and size spelled success, Doyle Dane's humorous "Think small" campaign for the low-priced German Volkswagen not only made its small size desirable but helped dispel its post–World War II reputation as a "Nazi" car. This striking and humorous synthesis of design and copy had rarely, if ever, been seen in advertising.

With the creation of art director–copywriter teams, the status of the art director was elevated. Whereas the art director had most often merely executed the copywriter's ideas, the art director was now an equal partner in the creative process. McCaffrey and McCall's Jack Sidebotham remembers starting at Young & Rubicam after World War II working in the pasteup room doing "mechanicals"—

mounting type and artwork on boards to provide an accurate guide for production into actual advertising. "Y&R," says Sidebotham, "was considered a haven for art directors then. Everybody started out doing pasteups but every other week you had the opportunity to leave the pasteup room and work with a full art director in his office. But even there, the traffic department delivered a piece of copy and the art director would then make a layout. He wouldn't even see the writer."

Today, as equal partners, art directors have as much say in the development of advertising as copywriters. They often have more outside contacts, as they work closely with photographers, suppliers, and the production houses that film and produce commercials. As one art director jokingly says: "You see the culmination of that at Christmastime when the art directors receive bottles of wine and the copywriters get nothing."

Creatives used to be relatively invisible within agencies. Even as enlightened an agency as Doyle Dane Bernbach kept its copywriters and art directors away from clients, relying upon the account group for client communication and contact. David Herzbrun says: "Creatives never even saw the client except perhaps the first couple of times out to get to know the background and maybe visit the factory. Maybe as time went on, you'd see the client in a sales meeting but the account guy would always go out with the campaign. We never presented our own work. He would come back having sold the work to the client or, if not, with the reasons why."

Although the situation varies from agency to agency, today even the least experienced copywriters and art directors frequently present their own work to the client. Creatives must know how to defend their work, explaining how it fits the strategy, solves the problem, and why it will work. Al Greenberg, a former creative director at Wells, Rich,

Greene and now chairman of the advertising-design department at Parsons School of Design, explains: "This is a people business. You must be able to sell what you produce. One of our most important tasks is to teach students to articulate what they have done and why."

Don Blauweiss, a senior vice president at Saatchi & Saatchi and on the faculty of Parsons School of Design, says, "Advertising is about selling. You are trying to move a product. Including your own." And George Lois, a Doyle Dane Bernbach alumnus, currently chairman-creative director of Lois Pitts Gershon Pon/GGK and one of the most influential and respected art directors in the business, said in a 1984 lecture at the School for Visual Arts, "A lot of your job is going to war. If you are talented, you spend a lot of time preserving, rationalizing, explaining, bullshitting your work. One percent of your time is inspiration, nine percent perspiration, and ninety percent justification. You must get good at selling your work and have joy in selling it."

Some agencies have reputations as being either "account driven" or "creative driven," meaning that one department is perceived as having more power than the other. The truth is that agencies are usually reflective of their major clients' management style. A large full-service agency that represents primarily package-goods accounts is likely to have a strong account group paralleling the internal structure of the client organization.

Within agencies, creative groups may differ in style depending upon the clients they service. For example, those who work on the Wendy's account at DFS/Dorland feel that their group is unique within the agency, a pocket of free-wheeling ideas where a certain amount of outrageousness is encouraged. At J. Walter Thompson, the same is true for those who work on Burger King, whereas those who work on

Thompson's Warner-Lambert account feel more constrained. The nation's thirteenth largest advertiser, Warner-Lambert spends almost $440 million among the eleven advertising agencies handling its many products, including Trident chewing gum, Listerine Antiseptic, Schick shavers, Sinutab, Certs, and Bubblicious Bubble Gum (statistics from *Advertising Age*). Like other package-goods companies, Warner-Lambert does not take a whimsical approach toward advertising its products, relying heavily upon its agencies' research and account-services departments.

Ultimately, top management determines an agency's style. J. Walter Thompson, Ogilvy & Mather, and Young & Rubicam are among the nation's largest agencies, servicing major package-goods accounts. Yet among creatives they have reputations as being good places to work, with creative supervisors who offer support and inspiration when ideas are not easily forthcoming or even on target.

Some agencies have reputations for routinely pitting creative teams against one another, giving them identical assignments and deadlines under which to come up with ideas. One copywriter says: "Creatives hate this. It's called a 'gangbang,' and is very demoralizing. It's one thing if you are working on a new-business presentation and need several concepts and campaigns. Also, there are deadlines and pressures that sometimes make it necessary. But where it happens all the time, you feel that the agency is saying: 'You're just here to service.' A good agency tries very hard to make it comfortable for you to create."

Working for an agency that understands and is committed to the creative process makes a great difference in the quality of the work produced. Jack Sidebotham states, "There are fairly clear distinctions between agencies that creative people like to work in and don't like to. You have a sense whether people really care how something looks or sounds. In the final analysis, people do better work in supportive environments."

When he was appointed Young & Rubicam's New York executive director, John Ferrell reorganized the agency's creative department. In an *ADWEEK* interview, he explained: "I have really concentrated on two things since I've had the job: the people who do the work and the environment they do the work in. My philosophy is, I am going to let the great work happen. If you give them the right environment that encourages freedom to be adventurous and to be the best they can, the people will drive themselves to do spectacular work."

Art directors and copywriters don't just create ads. As part of the entire group working on a client's business, they are involved in developing strategy. Jack Sidebotham says, "When I first started in this business, an account guy would come back from Ohio and say, 'This is what Goodyear wants us to do.' And, unless you were at a very senior level in the agency, you would never even see the client, much less talk about what the advertising should be. Today, unless you are dealing with one of those rare clients who just hands down a fiat and tells you to do what you are told, creatives get involved at the beginning."

Although copywriters and art directors sometimes feel that clients, and often the account group as well, rely too much upon research, most of the time there is positive collaboration among creative, account, and the client in creating the advertising. Messner et al.'s Ron Berger says of creatives and research, "Market research is an invaluable tool. To do good advertising, you must get answers to certain questions that you can only get from research. Who are you talking to? What do they want to hear? What are they interested in? Why are they interested in the product? Why aren't they interested? Why are they buying a competitive product?

"But the creative person is the one who does the advertising. We have to listen to the client and be able to articulate the client's need to ourselves. I don't think you can just get the information from the account person. Sometimes a client says something that he doesn't believe to be important, and suddenly I see that it is the key to the entire campaign. You have to be there when the foundation is poured and not just appear when the work is started."

When creative develops advertising, the client must give approval before the concepts can be produced. The usual procedure for getting advertising approval is for the account and creative groups to agree on the advertising and then, together, present it to the client. The approval process, however, can be frustrating, particularly for the copywriters and art directors who have worked so hard. As Ron Berger says, "One of the things that is toughest for creative people is the loss of a sense of authorship on their work." On package-goods accounts, in particular, there are often so many client levels through which the advertising must pass that by the time it gets to the uppermost level for final approval, the advertising is totally different from what was originally conceived.

Clients are in a difficult position as well. They say that they want creative, innovative advertising but they are often reluctant to take risks, particularly since hundreds of thousands of dollars may well be spent by the time the ad is produced and television time purchased. In addition, there is often unstated pressure on each person to whom the advertising is presented to make a change or suggestion—otherwise they may not be perceived as making a contribution.

Creatives feel caught in the middle of this. They see their work chopped up until the final version bears little resemblance to what was first suggested. Worse, if the product doesn't increase its market share or if it fails, the client often says it was the fault of the advertising.

As it happens, that just might be true—but for a very different reason. The best way to kill a bad product is to advertise it. Good advertising persuades consumers to try a product or a service. But after the first use, if the goods are bad and the purchaser dissatisfied, all the advertising in the world won't make for repeat use or purchase.

From the creative point of view, the best kind of client is one in which a single person makes the decision about the advertising. "You can almost make a correlation," says Ron Berger. "The more access you have to the decision makers, the better the advertising. Frank Perdue of Perdue Farms, Fred Pressman of Barney's, Stanley Kravetz of Timberland—these are the people who run their businesses and make decisions about the advertising. Nobody says that they are necessarily easy clients but the work they get is very good. At package-goods companies, you go through brand managers on up through senior management, and by the time you get to the chairman, what started off as a very good commercial has gone through twenty people and is now often fighting for its life."

Expanding on this, Jack Sidebotham comments, "A good client is one who is decisive. Even if he looks at your storyboard and says, 'That's a terrible piece of work, get out of my office,' you know where you are. I can understand someone who sees a campaign that you've worked on for a couple of months and says, 'I'm going to call you tomorrow. I have to think this over.' But too often you get this immediate 'That's terrific' from someone, and the next day he calls you up and

82

says: 'Change this and change that,' and the whole thing begins to peter out. It's hard and it happens a lot."

CREATING ADS

A creative could probably sell the client's product almost as well as the client's own sales force. Creatives visit the factory, sample and use the product, speak to technical research people, go to stores to see how the product is displayed, and listen to consumer focus groups talk about what they think about the product and why they do or do not use it.

This attention to detail is essential, and not only for creating individual ads or campaigns. An effective campaign creates an image of the product or service, one that is generally perceived to be independent of the advertising but is actually a result of it. In most Western nations, particularly the United States, consumers must choose among an overwhelming number of products and services. In the New York metropolitan area alone, there are over a dozen different long-distance telephone companies to choose from and forty-one varieties of hair mousse available in drugstores and supermarkets. With such a selection of services and products, all of them nearly equal, brand image or personality is a key sales component.

J. Walter Thompson researcher Alan Levine says: "Every product has a personality. If products were people, consumers would like and become friends with some, admire others, and shy away from certain ones. A lot of the work done in advertising is to create a brand personality."

Most creative assignments aren't even based upon new advertising strategies. Effective campaigns require maintenance. A lot of creative work consists of doing what are called "pool-outs," different executions of the same creative strategy. For instance, each commercial in the American Express "Do you know me?" campaign, which features as a central theme people with well-known names but little-known faces explaining how they use the American Express card, is a pool-out. Within the business, there is a consensus that a campaign that works should never be abandoned without good reason. If an advertising campaign is successful, it is reflected in sales; but it also means that the less quantifiably measured brand personality is appealing to consumers.

When effective, campaigns themselves become identified with the product. The just-mentioned American Express campaign is among these, as is the "Marlboro man," who has been on the range for over a quarter of a century. The "lonely Maytag repairman" has been waiting for the phone to ring for almost twenty years, and the Merrill Lynch bull led the herd for thirteen years before being dropped in 1985. These images remain viable and effective for years. However, even when a campaign continues to be successful, creatives work on new strategic executions to have in place if it becomes apparent that the campaign is wearing out.

When creatives begin to work on a new campaign, regardless of whether the advertising is to be placed in print, radio, or television, the groundwork is the same. In an *Advertising Age* interview, creative consultant Joe Sacco mentions a small sign that was displayed in a Doyle Dane Bernbach office for years: "Information is the source material for inspiration."

This is true for all creatives, whether they are working on package-goods accounts, service, or other types of accounts. Although it is considered important for professional advancement to have experience in all types of business, creatives often divide themselves into two types—those who enjoy working on package-goods accounts and those who don't. It depends upon the writer's personality. Package-goods accounts usually call for a systematic approach to the advertising, showing how using the product will provide a consumer benefit. Service and other types of accounts tend to attract writers who like to play with words, use humor, and generally break rules and take risks.

Copywriter Jean Campbell has worked on package-goods accounts at William Esty. Discussing how she approaches a new campaign, she says, "To write advertising, you must work off facts. You don't just go off and write flowery creative things. Before I even begin to think about creating the ad, I want to know everything there is to know about the product. I get facts from the account and research groups and go to the marketplace and look to see what's out on the shelves and how similar products are displayed. I try to find out everything about that product category—what the competition is doing, what has been done in the past, what has worked and what hasn't.

"When I was working on Nabisco Premium Saltine Crackers, I went to the Nabisco bakery to see how the crackers were made. I talked to the bakers and the Nabisco research people. I found out everything there is to know about making crackers—the ingredients, how they are baked, what the competition uses. When I worked on MasterCard, I had to learn how the card is marketed and about computers, particularly about a new computer system for the card. There were endless meetings and I was learning terms that nobody else in the agency could possibly understand. But from knowing everything, I could write the ad.

"Advertising is like crawling into people's heads and discovering what makes them tick. The end result may be just a slogan or tag line, but you can't write it unless you know to whom you are talking, what makes your product different, and what you want the advertising to do."

In its tiered structure, the creative department typically mirrors other agency departments. At the top is the creative director, although many agencies have two co–creative directors, one a writer and the other an art director. Large agencies are divided into groups, each led by a group head or co–group heads and consisting of copywriters and art directors. Each group is assigned its own accounts.

Art director and copywriter usually work together from the beginning of a project. Small agencies often don't formally assign copywriter/art director teams, instead permitting a process of selection based on compatibility and availability. Others, particularly the larger agencies, match writers and art directors.

When a team clicks, it can be magic. But when it doesn't it can be awkward. One writer says, "It's like a bad marriage." An art director says, "Personality and talent are important but compatibility is crucial. A really good team makes each of you better than you would be alone." When a team works well together, even radio commercials can be collaborative. One writer says: "My art director and I sit down together to talk about how we want the listener to picture what I will be writing."

Although print, television, and radio are different media requiring different creative skills and involvement, the first step in each is to isolate the *concept*, the key idea on which the ad is to be based. Ron Berger says, "In the beginning, the team comes up with the concept, which is basically the headline, and talks about how the ad is going to look. For a television ad, we never leave one another. We usually write the dialogue together and are there through casting, recording, and all of postproduction. But with print, we separate after we get the concept settled. I write the ad and the art director takes care of putting it together."

Gerry O'Hara, an art director at Ephron, Raboy, Tsao & Kurnit, says, "The copywriter/art director team functions best in developing the concept. We keep thinking about what we are trying to accomplish. If it is corporate advertisement, in which the goal is to get the company's name across, we try to convey something memorable about the corporate personality and character. If we are working on a fashion account, we must break through the clutter of all other fashion ads. If it's a tax-free bond, we work to grab that part of the consumer's brain that thinks about investments and the future. You must be serious but you must also be brash enough to break through all the other financial advertisements.

"We usually start with headline ideas. A headline should contain the news—the essence of the sell. I frequently have the idea for the headline but the copywriter can state it in words that better express its intentions. The same thing happens with visual ideas from the copywriter. Once we reach a consensus, we split up. The copywriter begins to work on the actual text, and I start to design. But we still go back and forth."

Television Ads

Although the majority of advertising dollars are spent on television production and the purchase of time in which the spots are aired, only large clients can afford television advertising on a regular basis. Small businesses do create spots that are usually aired over local television stations rather than a national network, but practically all television production is done by the large urban-based agencies that service major corporate clients. These agencies have special departments that oversee and coordinate production (see chapter 7).

Most creatives would rather work on television than any other kind of advertising. It is considered by many to be the glamour part of the advertising business. A reel containing good television spots adds value to a creative's worth that print alone rarely does; TV experience is important for career advancement. Copywriters and art directors learn on the job, beginning with what one writer calls the "schlep work"—things like coupon ads, trade ads (ads for products directed toward retailers and wholesalers rather than consumers), and promotional pieces. As they progress, creatives move on to print campaigns, radio, and television commercials.

Most creatives find it easier to work on television advertising than print. Throughout the entire process, television is collaborative so responsibility gets shared. Although television is often more time-consuming than print and demands constant creative attention throughout each step of production, creatives working on television are simply not as vulnerable as those working on print. Not only is the creation of print advertising essentially a solitary process, but the print ad must stand alone. There are many ways to make a television spot work that don't just involve copy and design; these include music, sound effects, or humorous actions. Whereas print requires both conceptual and applied skill in either writing or art, television is basically conceptual.

In addition, many feel that it is easier to sell television advertising ideas to clients than to sell print. Ron Berger, who enjoys print and has won awards for his work for Timberland, says: "It's harder to deal with the client in print. Every word and sentence can be analyzed, whereas with television, criticism seems to go away a lot faster."

In its early days, television was still a copywriter's medium. Commercials were performed live at the television studios in front of a camera. Usually a pitchman stood before the camera and talked about or demonstrated the product. When commercial production became an agency function, the role of the art director changed. Today many television spots are almost exclusively visual, using music instead of words, with perhaps just a brief tag line at the end. New technology has made formerly difficult and expensive visual effects much easier to achieve. Global marketing has created an emphasis on visual rather than talking commercials, as visuals are effective in crossing language and cultural barriers.

The transition from print to television during the 1950s was not easy for many art directors. Jack Sidebotham, who was the first head of the television art department at Young & Rubicam, says: "Some art directors resisted television because the end product was not absolutely under their control. An art director working with print can fiddle with things like type, its arrangement, choosing a photo or illustration and its position and placement. Television is more collaborative, with many different people involved throughout the various steps of production."

An art director working on a television commercial no longer functioned primarily as a graphic designer. Conceptual skills became more important. Today's television art director is a filmmaker as well as a designer. He must understand editing and what can be achieved using tape and film. An art director working in television sets a graphic tone to the work, but the final work is executed by the director who films the spot.

The art director and copywriter develop the television spot and present it as a storyboard, a panel containing illustrations of the various shots to be filmed and the dialogue to be spoken by the actors subtitled on each shot. Marty Muller, an art director at J. Walter Thompson, describes the process of developing television ads: "The copywriter and I sit down together and think how to execute the idea in terms of fifteen-, thirty-, or sixty-second television commercials. We think frame by frame. We keep asking questions like, What is the action? What is this stand-up pitch guy going to do with his hand? What are the background details that will illustrate our idea? We either write together and both decide on the visuals, or we separate and the copywriter writes and I start laying out the ad. At some point soon, though, we get back together and make changes. A lot of the time, I take my pad and work in her office or she brings her notebook in here."

Print Ads

Creatives usually have strong feelings about print. They either love it or hate it. All, however, find it difficult. "The most intimidating thing that I do," says Ron Berger, "is to sit down and write the print ad. I find I often spend days writing a single ad. You have to capture the emotion and attitude about the product in print in such a way that the ad sounds like it's talking to you rather than writing to you. You can't hide it. It sits there and if it's not right, everytime you read it, it will grate on you. That's not true with television. You can cover with music, a funny actor, or any number of other things."

Talking about her approach to print, William Esty's Jean Campbell says: "While I am gathering all the information, I am thinking about what I must do. I let the ideas crystallize. Sometimes it takes a lot of time, but I know they will come. Sometimes it's a matter of regurgitating all the facts and ideas I can think of, almost as if I must clear my mind of everything that won't work in order to get to that next level of, Oh, that seems good or, That may be right." Writer Julie Begel, formerly at Venet Advertising, says: "You wrap your head around something and try to think how you feel about it. You personalize it, relate it to your life."

Art director Gerry O'Hara, by choice, works almost entirely on print. When he creates print ads, he says, "I always remember that people see before they read. You have to stop them with the visual. I always try to create an ad in which all the visual components, including type, photography, layout, and graphics, work together to communicate the idea behind the ad. It all boils down to getting someone to stop, look, and remember the message you are trying to put across. I am trying to give a product or a company a personality that will be remembered."

At many agencies, print has been downplayed in importance, often relegated to junior writers. But, after years in which television dominated, there is a returning emphasis on creative print advertising. Some agencies, including D'Arcy MacManus & Masius, Rosenfeld Sirowitz & Humphrey, and Benton & Bowles, are even offering seminars and support groups for writers who may not feel confident writing for print.

Radio Ads

Radio spots must capture a listener's attention. Ideally, the listener creates his own visualization of the person speaking or the product being spoken about or becomes involved in a story. Copywriters tend to enjoy doing radio spots although, says Julie Begel, "With television, you are working with so many people, all of whom can help to see that it works. But with radio, you are really all by yourself. Until you go into production and get your actors and perhaps the music track in the background, you are all alone."

One thing that creatives don't particularly like about working on radio spots is presenting them. Layouts are used for print, and storyboards for television. But radio, which relies on sound only, is frequently presented by the writer alone—who not infrequently feels self-conscious "performing" it. To avoid this, many writers and agencies present radio commercials in demo recording form.

JOBS

Although agencies have been hiring experienced art directors and copywriters in record numbers during the past few years, even offering perks like summer houses, private-school tuitions for children, and special health plans, it is more difficult to attain an entering position in the creative department than in any other agency area (with the possible exception of television production). There are entry-level positions for art directors, who can work in the agency's art studio, or "bullpen," preparing material for final production at the engraver. But it is hardest for beginning writers, although the situation is easing up somewhat, particularly out of New York City.

One copywriter, now working at Grey Advertising, says: "Next to being an actor, it's probably the next most impossible job to get. There are no beginning writer jobs." Another writer, at Bozell, Jacobs, Kenyon & Eckhardt, says: "It's difficult to break in. Most agencies have no use for people that they have to train. They don't want to pay you in order to teach you. I finally got hired when I agreed to take a secretarial position with a small agency and was promised some writing on the side. It turned out to be a good solution because I wasn't under pressure to produce; and, within seven months I became a writer." According to a senior vice president at Lord, Geller, Federico & Einstein, the agency has doctorate and master's degree recipients working as receptionists and secretaries, many hoping for an entry into the creative department.

In the larger agencies, people are usually hired to work within a group that services one or more accounts. Most agencies move junior copywriters and art directors from one group to another so that budding creatives can get experience on a variety of business. Agencies pay beginners starting salaries of about $18,000, although the figure varies greatly according to agency size and location.

This is slowly changing as agencies are finding it increasingly difficult to find good copywriters. According to *AD-WEEK*, copywriters' salaries are up about 50 percent in the past five years, reflecting the demand. Some agencies are actually recruiting on college campuses and have even started or revived training programs for entry-level writers. Among those agencies are McKinney Silver & Rockett (Raleigh, North Carolina), Ogilvy & Mather (New York), Young & Rubicam (New York), DFS/Dorland (New York), and J. Walter Thompson (New York).

However, most agencies prefer to hire someone with experience and do not have the specific training programs for creatives that they have on the account side. As one agency spokesperson states: "Junior people in account management and media can be kept busy as coordinators or number crunchers. Creatives must produce client-ready work, so there is no way to use them in training."

Almost without exception, aspiring copywriters and art directors must have a portfolio in order to be considered for an agency position. Called a "book," a presentable portfolio is maintained by even the most senior people. As one moves from doing only print ads to television, the book will also include a "reel," a videotape with samples of television commercials.

The portfolio for a beginning copywriter or art director trying to break in should include hypothetical single ads, as well as advertising campaigns, which are several ads or commercials tied together by a single concept. A book should include ads for package goods, hard goods such as home appliances or computers, food or fashion, public service or tourism, and new products. There should be at least three campaigns including television, print, radio, and outdoor billboards, with several different approaches included, such as music, testimonials, and demonstration. It's a good idea to include at least one campaign for package goods.

An art director should include headlines for all ads because art directors will be expected to come up with headlines on the job. Additional copy is fine but not necessary. Writers should not only include headlines but descriptive body as well. If you are a writer who cannot draw, primitive line drawings or stick figures are perfectly acceptable. Many people do get help from artist friends or even hire an artist to help prepare their books. But it is important that it be clear that all concepts, ideas, and material are those of the writer alone and not the product of a collaboration.

George Lois, speaking about portfolios in an *ADWEEK* interview, says, "Make sure you have ideas. The ads themselves don't have to be professional. No one wants to look at another dumb *Time* magazine ad. It's the bright ideas that we want. And don't worry. Someone will see your talent. Keep at it until you get a break."

Those who do the hiring look for evidence of a type of

conceptual thinking that reflects some feeling for the way in which advertising is created. Skill isn't as important as ideas. A beginning copywriter at Grey says, "I was told that they would rather hire people who had far-out ideas and reel them in when it was necessary." Another beginner, at DFS/ Dorland, says, "They want to see incredible stuff in the spec book—wild, inventive, intuitive, interesting material. But when you get the job, you aren't asked to do that."

Students of advertising-design programs generally have a completed portfolio at graduation but many people get into advertising who have not attended advertising programs. As a matter of fact, Jack Sidebotham speaks for most agencies when he says, "You hire people on potential. There aren't too many schools that train specifically and turn out a good finished product. A couple of months in the bullpen and someone learns more than in four years of school. I'd rather have someone study something like Chinese history and take a couple of ad courses and then come and learn details on the job."

Help or advice with portfolio preparation is available to the beginning copywriter or art director. *How to Put Your Book Together and Get a Job in Advertising*, by Maxine Paetro (Executive Communications, 919 Third Avenue, New York, New York 10022; the cost is $9.95, plus $1.25 postage), is a very readable primer on portfolio preparation and contains general information on the creative job search. The Art Directors Club, the One Club, and the Society of Illustrators (see Appendix: Getting a Job in Advertising) offer one-to-one consultations between experienced and fledgling creatives. These organizations can also be helpful in recommending courses or schools in your area that have courses on portfolio preparation.

Possibly the best recent news for aspiring creatives was

expressed by Steve Bowen and James B. Patterson, respectively general manager and creative director of J. Walter Thompson in New York. According to them, many clients are seeking more creative, even risk-taking, advertising. As a result, the demand for talented creatives is increasing.

In an effort to open the door (and perhaps to get some publicity as well), J. Walter Thompson purchased a full-page ad in the November 30, 1984, edition of the *New York Times* in which eight copywriting assignments were given to aspiring copywriters under the heading, "Write if you want work." Assignments ranged from "The ingredients listed on the tin of baked beans reads: 'Beans, Water, Tomatoes, Sugar, Salt, Modified Starch, Vinegar, Spices.' Make it sound mouthwatering" to "Describe, in not more than 100 words, the plot of the last episode of 'Dynasty.'" The test offered the best respondents the opportunity to be employed as trainee copywriters at the agency.

Over 1,600 people sent in responses. The agency interviewed twenty-two people and hired nine, all of whom were in their twenties, with the exception of Chuck Hoffman, a forty-three-year-old English teacher at a New York City high school who gave up a salary of more than $30,000 a year to take a position as a junior copywriter at a salary of about $18,000. During the summer of 1986, J. Walter Thompson revived the ad as part of a new college recruitment effort.

There is a lot of career movement in advertising, particularly in the beginning years. Columnist Ed Buxton estimates that the turnover in the creative departments at Kenyon & Eckhardt and Compton since the 1950s has been 400 or 500 percent, meaning that each creative position has been filled by four to five people. As he wrote in his *ADWEEK* column, "For all practical purposes, there is no such thing as a full career for creative people in any one agency." Many believe movement to be the only way to increase salary and gain a better position. One copywriter says: "People wonder if you stay somewhere too long. You just can't play it safe and expect to be any kind of star."

Everybody in the business knows immediately when someone has worked on a "hot" ad or campaign, and it is not uncommon for an up-and-coming copywriter or art director to receive an "Are you interested in talking with us?" call from another agency within weeks of beginning a new position. Headhunters and agency personnel directors who wouldn't even glance at the beginner's book are suddenly wooing him on the telephone.

This can be a problem. "There are people," says Ron Berger, "who build reputations on a single ad or commercial. That's the down side of this business. I think that it's analogous to the sports industry. There are athletes who have one very good season and end up signing a multiyear contract for millions of dollars. But then they never duplicate that season's performance again. The same thing happens in this business. If the timing is right and you win awards, you can milk that for the rest of your career."

There are some, however, who question the wisdom of too much movement. Ogilvy & Mather's Fran Devereux says, "I think you should change jobs sometimes. But if you know that you are on a fast track, even if you feel you are treading water for a while, it's often worth hanging in. There's nothing in this business that replaces long-term relationships."

6

Media

Although not as well known to most people as the account-services, creative, or research departments, an agency's media department performs one of advertising's most important tasks. For it is the media department that must obtain the best and most effective possible exposure for the client's advertising, as well as insure that it appears before the right audience. Creative may come up with brilliant advertising that is based upon the solid findings of the research department, but if that advertising doesn't appear before the appropriate buying public, it is useless.

The media task sounds deceptively easy. Media planners develop yearly media plans for clients that list each media outlet—print, outdoor display, and broadcast—on which the advertising will be placed. In most agencies, the media department is divided into two subdepartments: planning and buying. In addition to preparing media plans, planners purchase print space; buyers purchase broadcast time.

Media planning and buying used to be fairly routine. Within agencies, the media department was too often viewed as a place where number-crunching clerks figured out how to attain the lowest CPM, or cost per thousand, for clients. CPM is a basic media concept and represents the cost of reaching one thousand people, homes, or some other designated unit to whom the advertising message is directed. It is a means whereby advertisers can calculate the true cost of reaching the desired audience for the ads.

Today, though, sophisticated data-gathering systems identify consumer groups and collect market demographic information with an accuracy and depth unimaginable just a few years ago. Numbers and calculations that formerly took hours are now completed within seconds by computers, freeing planners to concentrate on strategic planning. Today's media planner must be a sophisticated marketer who understands consumer needs and desires and can match these to appropriate media choices—of which there are, today, a vast array.

Media has become one of advertising's most exciting and challenging areas. For example, research has shown that, until fairly recently, virtually all automobiles were purchased by men. Research indicated as much concern among buyers, although not necessarily consciously, in the image conveyed by their automobile as in its performance. Based upon this information, creative consistently developed advertising that emphasized speed and looks and implied (not always subtly) that the purchase of a particular model would satisfy these underlying psychological as well as transportation needs.

In 1964, commercials introducing the Ford Mustang juxtaposed the image of a white mustang galloping along a beach with the image of a young man sitting behind the wheel of the new automobile, an attractive woman beside him. The planner who selected the media on which the Mustang spots were to appear undoubtedly knew that Sunday night had—as it continues to have—a higher proportion of male television viewers than any other night and, further, that sports programs get the largest available male audience. That media planner didn't have to think too hard before choosing sixty seconds on a network television Sunday night sports special over which to air the automobile spot.

Today it is not so simple. Both societal values and media possibilities have changed dramatically. Condé Nast Publications, which annually surveys the women's market, shows that women are buying new cars in significant numbers. Women's magazines such as *McCalls* and *Ms.* run features on car repair. Women actually purchase twenty models more than men do, including the Buick Skyhawk, Toyota Corolla, Oldsmobile Calais, and Mazda RX-7. Morover, women tend to be more rational and less emotional about choosing automobiles. They are concerned about safety and performance, and they respond to different commercial messages than men. Advertisers must now appeal to a multiplicity of car-buying publics. It is the job of the media department to work with account and research, first to identify these diverse buying publics and then to recommend the best advertising outlets by which to reach multiple audiences.

In addition to network and local television and conventional print media, media specialists must consider a vast array of media possibilities, including cable television, international television beamed via satellite, VCRs, shop-at-home television services, syndication, and barter syndication (in which a local television station gives a television packager commercial time instead of cash as payment for a show). For instance, in early 1986, Procter & Gamble began offering local independent television stations a movie package called "Platinum 193," consisting of made-for-television films from the 1970s. Stations aired the movies and, instead of paying cash, gave Procter & Gamble 10½ minutes of commercial time each week.

Changes in the media field extend beyond the media task itself. Agency media departments are today in competition with outside media-buying services and with clients themselves, who may be assuming their own media-planning and buying functions. This trend has significant implications for advertising agencies. The media department is often responsible for spending millions of dollars of the client's money. Clients monitor performance as never before and agencies must therefore pay more attention to their media departments. Since the 15 percent commission received by an agency on all media purchases almost always represents the largest share of agency revenues, this is serious business. Agency media departments are under pressure to come up with innovative, effective, and cost-efficient service. For example, Joseph E. Seagram & Sons recently took about $55 million in billings from its agencies to set up House of Seagram Media, an in-house media planning and buying service that handles all Seagram media activity with the exception of broadcast.

In the past fifteen years, over one hundred autonomous media-buying companies have been formed. Some of these provide media services for small agencies who don't have their own media-buying departments; but others handle major accounts from clients who prefer these outside media services to those of their agencies.

MEDIA PLANNING

Media planners are members of the client's marketing team. Planners, along with the account group, meet with the client to develop marketing objectives and to identify the client's niche in the marketplace. Just as market and creative research provide the foundation on which to base advertising strategy, media research provides demographic facts about the various media. In many agencies, media planners advise creatives about new media possibilities that may call for different creative skills and thinking.

Simply stated, the media plan is a document, often over 150 pages long, that lists all of the media on or in which a client's advertising is to be placed. The plan includes the goals of the advertising, an explanation as to why and how the media plan will successfully meet these goals, a description of the target audience, a statement of the media strategy, the rationale for selecting certain media, and costs. The media plan contains charts, graphs, analysis of television time slots (which are called *parts* and are separated into day, nighttime, late night, and weekend), and a discussion of the types of shows and publications planners believe will be most effective in reaching the target audience. Together, annual media plans provide a source for a complete advertising history of a specific brand or service.

Talking about media planning, Steve Zigler, former head of media planning at Wells, Rich, Greene, and now the owner of an antique store in the Berkshires, says: "When we receive the marketing direction on the brand and the client's advertising budget, the first thing we do is to define the target audience. In order to do this, we must know both demographics—age, income, education, family status, occupation—and psychographics—life-style and attitudes.

"We must know a product's seasonality in order to determine the best times in which to advertise. Toothpaste is purchased all year and has no special season. But other products are purchased at certain times a year, such as cameras, which sell most strongly right before Christmas and Easter.

"We find out where our users live—the geography. Even a so-called national brand isn't really part of a national market. Geographic areas are very distinct and each market is different because of demographic and psychographic influences and the competition in the marketplace.

"Media planners decide, as well, both how many people the advertising must reach in order to provide a base of sales and the number of times they must be exposed to the message in order to raise awareness. Advertising doesn't register immediately. In order for the content of an ad or commercial to become meaningful to the target audience, the message must be repeated."

Reach and *frequency* are key media terms. Reach is the total number of people who have been exposed to a message at least once during a set time period (usually four weeks). Frequency is the average number of times that the population was exposed during that period of time. Reach and frequency usually require a trade-off. As reach goes up, frequency goes down. It is usually cost-prohibitive to establish both a high reach and a high frequency.

For example, in June 1985, when Chevrolet introduced the Nova, planners decided that frequency was more important than reach, but that a reasonable balance of reach and frequency could be achieved—by concentrating initial advertising efforts in 129 markets between the Rockies and the Appalachians. Therefore, the media plan called for saturation of this limited geographic area rather than infrequent ads over a larger area. According to *Marketing and Media Decisions*, the plan laid out full-color newspaper ads in the top ten markets of that geographic area and black-and-white ads in 193 dailies and 128 weeklies during the week of Chevrolet's June 13 official announcement of the Nova. There were spot television buys throughout the 129 markets beginning June 1 that would preannounce the new automobile and then continue through August. Outdoor ads were placed in the top five markets.

Although it sounds as if advertising time and space is purchased following the clear instructions set forth in the media plan, it is not quite so simple. Media specialists continually recommend buys that will best accomplish the media objectives and yet reflect continuing changes in both the client's product or service and the media over which the message appears. Airlines, which in this age of deregulation, constantly change fares and compete with one another with special promotions and giveaways, are notoriously difficult accounts in this respect. As one media planner who works on the Pan Am account says, "We operate within the guidelines of the media plan but things are never set. We are selling a service that is changing nonstop twenty-four hours a day, seven days a week. And while we are trying to get the client the best exposure possible, we must always know what the client has spent, what the client has left to spend, and where we can best spend what's left."

MEDIA BUYING: PRINT

In most agencies, planners buy space in print media in addition to planning the client's yearly media activities. There are resource publications—primarily *Standard Rate and Data*, the bible of print—that supply facts about periodicals, their size, advertising rates, and dates of special issues and supplements. Newspapers and magazines also publish annual rate cards and media packets that tell planners: a publication's circulation; the number of copies of each issue distributed; its primary audience, which is the number of readers who buy or subscribe; and the secondary audience, which is those who see the publication without actually purchasing it. For instance, *People* has a circulation of almost 2.8 million but its total audience is more than 21 million.

Magazines and newspapers have representatives ("reps") who, as the term implies, represent their publications to advertisers. They are salespeople, knowledgeable about their publications' statistics and readership information, and they can be very helpful to media planners. "You learn to be real nice to reps," says one planner, "and reps learn to be nice to you. You want positioning, and they want our business."

Not all publications have reps. Small publications often use the services of media-rep firms to represent them at agencies. Sometimes a large advertising agency ends up going directly to a small-town newspaper or publication in order to reach a certain target group.

Prices for television and radio time are negotiable because a fixed amount of inventory exists: the station's time. Magazines and newspapers have expandable space: the more advertising space purchased, the more pages they can print. Therefore, print rates are theoretically fixed and print buyers cannot negotiate as do broadcast buyers.

MEDIA BUYING: BROADCAST

When television became an advertising vehicle during the 1950s, advertising agencies, as they had with radio, produced shows for clients who acted as sole sponsors. Among the most active agencies was BBDO, which produced three documentary drama series: "Armstrong Circle Theater," "General Electric Theater" (hosted by Ronald Reagan), and "The U.S. Steel Hour." General Foods' Maxwell House coffee underwrote the popular weekly family series "I Remember Mama," and Bristol-Myers's "Alfred Hitchcock Presents."

Sponsors were concerned primarily with the positive identification they received through their association with these shows. They stressed good production values and quality programming. General Foods ran its Maxwell House coffee commercials only at the start and finish of "I Remember Mama," allowing the show to run uninterrupted. Alcoa underwrote Edward R. Murrow's sometimes controversial "See It Now" broadcasts.

Sponsors did have their idiosyncrasies, though. When a contestant with the last name of "Ford" appeared on the Groucho Marx show, "You Bet Your Life," he was asked to use another name because the show was underwritten by DeSoto. On "The Goldbergs," a weekly series sponsored by General Foods, someone usually managed to drink a cup of Sanka, a General Foods product, during the telecast.

Eventually, the networks started to produce shows on their own. It became too expensive for one advertiser to support a single program, and the stage was set for today's business in which advertisers buy time, usually in sixty-, thirty-, and now fifteen-second increments. With the exception of Procter & Gamble, which produces daytime soaps through its agency Benton & Bowles, sole sponsorship of a regularly aired telecast is a thing of the past.

However, some advertisers are again producing and sponsoring television specials. It is attractive to sponsors because it gives them more control over the actual programming to which they lend their name, and hopefully adds to their prestige, as viewers associate the sponsor with the shows the sponsors choose to underwrite.

With production costs so high, only the largest advertisers can afford to consider this. According to an *ADWEEK* special report in November 1984, a made-for-television movie cost about $2.5 million to produce, plus almost $1 million to buy the broadcast time. The Chrysler Corporation financed and sponsored "The Last Days of Patton," broadcast by CBS in September 1986, and Apple Computer was sole sponsor of "Death of a Salesman," starring Dustin Hoffman, which aired on the same network in the fall of 1985.

Currently, even that overwhelming majority of advertisers who could not begin to fantasize about producing their own shows are attempting to exert more control over how they use television. This is because audiences are not watching network television the way they used to. According to *ADWEEK*, although usually about 73 percent of those viewers who have their televisions on at any one time are watching network television, this figure used to be closer to 90 percent and is expected to drop to 65 percent by 1990. As one media specialist points out, "Short of opening a new plant, television is ordinarily a client's biggest expense."

Whereas once ABC, NBC, and CBS were the only game in town, aside from some low-rated independent stations, viewers today have a wide choice of viewing options. These include cable television, public television, and the increasingly popular independent stations—which broadcast both original programming and shows in syndication, including such popular programs as "Donahue" and "Entertainment Tonight." According to *City Business*, New York City's three independent TV stations now attract more than 40 percent of the city's total viewing audience. These nonnetwork alternatives are called AOT, for "All Other Television."

Despite the erosion in network viewing, until the 1986 summer buying season, prices for network commercial time had continually risen, putting advertisers in the awkward position of paying more money for fewer viewers. Each year, the networks routinely upped the price of time, and sponsors had no choice but to pay. In 1986, however, for the first time, ABC and CBS actually dropped their prices, cutting about one percent from 1985 rates. NBC, the top-rated network, was nevertheless successful in raising its prices an average of 3 to 7 percent. According to *Advertising Age*, however, industry observers do not interpret this as a trend. Rather, most people believe that 1987 will see substantial price increases among all three major networks.

Clients and agencies work together to decide how media dollars are best spent. Within the media department, media buyers—or broadcast buyers, as they are increasingly called—purchase time over radio and television. Agencies divide buyers into network buyers and "spot" buyers, who purchase time in local markets. Just as with print, the broadcast buyer receives budgetary direction from the client and makes a determination about reach and frequency. The budget is then broken down so that television time can be purchased up front on a fifty-two-week basis, quarterly, or on a scatter basis allowing for last-minute, per-show purchases.

The basic value of a television program is determined by ratings and share. These ratings provide the basis on which networks price programs and sponsors measure their value. A network rating point represents one percent of all television households. It is the percentage of total possible audience. The share—short for "share of audience"—is a competitive evaluation that shows how a show rates against other programs broadcast at the same time. For instance, at the end of November 1985, "The Cosby Show," the NBC situation comedy starring Bill Cosby, was far and away the most popular regular show on television, registering an average 31.44 rating and a 42 share. This meant that more than 31 percent of all television owners were watching "The

Cosby Show" and that of all the people who had their televisions on during that time slot, 42 percent were watching the show.

Traditionally, two companies, the Arbitron Ratings Co. and the A. C. Nielsen Co., have collected data on television viewing, with Nielsen measuring national television audiences and Arbitron local markets. Through a computerized hookup to about 1,700 homes in eleven major markets, Nielsen collects viewing data each night that is tallied and delivered to agencies and networks. These are the "overnights," and they provide ratings on a daily basis. Another sample of homes fills out viewing diaries that provide demographic data as to exactly who in each home is watching which show at what time.

Four times a year, this same process is expanded to an additional 200 cities. This quarterly measurement is called the "sweeps" and is done in November, February, May, and July, although the July results are of minimal value because people don't watch nearly as much television in the summer. During sweeps months, networks upgrade their programming in order to drive up the ratings for their local affiliate stations. There is usually a rash of miniseries, movies, and entertainment specials during sweeps months as stations compete with one another for ratings points.

The television industry is today on the verge of a revolution in audience measurement. That revolution is arriving in the form of new ratings devices called "people meters." People meters have remote-control keypads that connect to television sets. Viewers press a specially assigned identifying number when they begin watching television and again when they stop. The meters provide continuous viewing information and, unlike the monitor/diary system, immediately link program and demographic information.

Nielsen statistics were still used as the basis for the 1986 up-front buying season but by 1987, people meters will most likely provide the foundation for network television buying. This has put the entire system in a state of flux and has created a particularly difficult situation for the networks. Although the networks put up most of the research money for the development of people meters, the earliest reports generated by the meters' use indicate that overall levels of television viewing are lower than previously reported. This will affect networks and advertisers in ways still to be seen.

Broadcast buyers rely on a combination of research, experience, and intuition. Since time over a show is purchased before the program is broadcast, buyers must forecast the value of that time in advance and then try to purchase it at the best possible price.

Spring marks the start of the major buying season and is, in the words of one buyer, "the time we work weekends and ten-hour days; and no one thinks of taking a day off until August." This is because each network issues its fall schedule in May and up-front buying begins in late June. Before they can begin to purchase a year's worth of programming, clients and agencies must decide how to allocate their television dollars.

Laura Nathanson, a network supervisor at BBDO, says: "Before I start spending maybe fifty million dollars for a client, I must know what we are doing. We examine how the client's shows did last year and if any didn't do what they were expected to do, we try to discover why. We develop strategies to best spend that money. Do we want it in prime time, daytime, or late time? Do we want to place it all up front or only seventy-five percent of it, holding money to use on a scatter basis?"

Major advertisers usually spend most of their money up front. Broadcast buyers purchase packages consisting of a variety of programs. For instance, a prime-time package might include some new programs that the agency believes will be successful, some continuing series of proven worth in terms of ratings, and perhaps some shows with low ratings but good demographics. Networks need that money up front; to encourage agency buys, they usually offer some kind of "make good" if the package doesn't deliver at the ratings stated by the television station. This is called a "guarantee."

What this means, points out John Sisk, head of network buying at J. Walter Thompson, is that it's "not difficult to be average in this business. Both the agencies and the networks have good research." But buyers hope to be in the enviable position of seeing a show or package on which time has been purchased come in at even a higher rating than was anticipated. "The rare thing," continues Sisk, "is the breakthrough—where you buy and even though it was guaranteed, you do better. That's where the kicks are."

Buyers don't buy time only according to the ratings. The demographic, or audience, composition is equally important. Advertisers sometimes pay more for a lower-rated show that appeals to the selected target audience than for a higher-rated show that might have more viewers. For instance, NBC's "Amazing Stories," Steven Spielberg's series, doesn't have nearly as many viewers as CBS's "Murder, She Wrote," which stars Angela Lansbury. But "Amazing Stories" attracts more viewers in the eighteen-to-forty-one age range, which is the target age group upon which most advertisers base their television buys. Therefore, advertisers spend the same for a thirty-second spot on each show.

Seasonality is taken into consideration as well, which is why money is frequently allocated for quarterly buying. Over-the-counter cold remedies have their greatest sales during the third quarter, which is January through March.

One media buyer says, "I've worked on accounts where someone comes in and says, 'There's a flu epidemic in Boston. Isn't that great?' and the spot-buying department immediately gets to work."

In addition, buyers purchase by the show. Broadcast buyers for Kodak managed to get three minutes over the 1986 Academy Awards telecast. Even at $1.8 million, this represented a real coup for the sponsor, as there is a waiting list among advertisers who want to purchase time over this popular telecast. However, most clients who retain money for scatter buys do so because there is the opportunity to get in on last-minute program vacancies, often for little money. This is where real negotiating skills come into play. As Laura Nathanson points out, "A lot of things are happening all the time. It's easy to get confused. You must know where you want to be, but also where you are willing to settle, and at what point the price gets so high you just say, 'See you,' and walk off."

Most broadcast buyers thrive on the action. "Last July," says John Sisk, "we placed about $250 billion in orders for our clients. That's an incredible high. You are working so hard and it's tense. Finally, you give the order to the network and you go, 'Whew, it's over,' but then you immediately feel down. This is a business with real highs and lows."

Says Laura Nathanson, "You always have the feeling when you close a deal that you should have done even better. You never stop working for your clients. It's always tense but it's also a lot of fun. You are on the phone all day talking to salespeople, clients, networks. It's being in the middle of everything and watching it all happen."

JOBS

As mentioned earlier, the good news for beginning media specialists is that agency media departments are changing. Agencies are upgrading the status of their media departments for two reasons. The diversity and sophistication of media possibilities have made clients and agencies much more dependent on the input of agency media departments. In addition, in order to hold onto their best media people, agencies must be competitive with independent media-buying and -planning organizations, which typically pay salaries 20 to 30 percent higher than agencies.

Reflecting this general trend, for example, BBDO has created a new unit called the Diversified Communications Group, in which the media department is given marketing responsibilities. At Benton & Bowles, media personnel work on single accounts along with researchers, creatives, and account personnel. This is true at Ogilvy & Mather as well. One planner there says, "Because there is a small group working on one account, it is easier to get a team spirit. A group concept heightens awareness of media involvement."

Detroit's Campbell-Ewald has restructured its media department so that its media personnel are "local market specialists." At most agencies, planners specialize in specific categories such as newspapers or trade publications, and buyers purchase for only one medium, such as spot television. In contrast, media people at Campbell-Ewald are responsible for all media, including newspapers, radio, television, and outdoor, in one specific market.

Whereas people frequently entered the media department as a stepping-stone to account management, this is not as common today. Some agencies have strict policies against allowing people to move from media into account work but others do permit interdepartmental moves. And despite media's old reputation as being a place of long hours for low pay, it is not easy to get media jobs. Agencies today intentionally hire people who will have ongoing contact with clients instead of relegating them to the back room. The head of media planning at one large agency estimates that he receives at least one hundred letters a month from aspiring employees; and, according to *Advertising Age*, in 1984, Chicago's Leo Burnett Company selected forty-five trainees from over eight thousand applicants. Average starting salaries range from $11,000 to $14,000.

Media trainees come from a variety of disciplines. In an informal survey of media departments, *Advertising Age* found that four preferred marketing/business majors, five preferred advertising majors, four preferred a mathematics background, and three preferred a computer-science background. In an interview before he left Wells Rich Greene, Steve Zigler, the former head of media planning, said, "I look for a solid math background, and the ability to write. Usually, you find that someone is strong in one and weak in the other. It's the balance that we need. I also suggest that everyone take two courses: an introduction to computers and a logic course, either the logic of statistics or systematic psychology. You must know how to think logically in this business and have the ability to distill a tremendous amount of information."

John Sisk says, "We like to bring people up through research. I look for two things: a good research background and the ability to present. We participate in new-business presentations and are constantly interacting with the client. Communications ability is really important."

More and more agencies are offering media beginners extensive training programs, although they vary from agency to agency. Young & Rubicam, J. Walter Thompson, Mc-Cann-Erickson, BBDO, Ted Bates, SSC & B, Needham, Harper Worldwide, and Ogilvy & Mather are among agencies that offer formal media training programs in addition to agency training programs. These programs vary in length but all cover media basics, presentation skills, research, buying, and planning for each medium, and require trainees to prepare a media plan.

PART THREE

The Advertising
Agency:
Support Departments

7

Production

Once the client approves the advertising, the creative material must be translated into usable form so that it can be sent to the media on or in which it is to appear. This is called production. In the larger agencies, production is divided into the broadcast- and print-production departments. There are so many details and expenses involved in producing a television spot that broadcast is subdivided with a separate department that assumes administrative and financial responsibilities, usually called broadcast operations or business affairs. Working closely with production and often under its umbrella as well is the traffic department, which schedules, supervises, and coordinates the work flow. Many agencies have separate departments for print and broadcast traffic.

Because the greatest share of advertising dollars is spent on television (over $15 billion in 1985), we will look at broadcast advertising in some depth.

BROADCAST

Before the advent of television, broadcast was restricted to radio. Advertising agencies actually owned and produced the majority of the most popular and widely listened-to radio shows for their clients. In 1949, when television was still a new medium and many still questioned its potential impact, advertisers spent only $12.3 million on television advertising. According to Stephen R. Fox in his book *The Mirror Makers*, just two years later, in 1951, there was no longer any doubt that this new medium was indeed the wave of the future, and television expenditures increased more than 1,000 percent to $128 million.

Television offered previously unimagined opportunities for clients and their agencies. A television viewer could actually see a product and how it worked. Newly influential television performers, like radio personalities before them, touted certain products, imparting their celebrity mystique to particular brands. Television was new and a source of fascination. In towns and neighborhoods throughout the nation, the news of a newly acquired television set spread like wildfire, and invitations from new television owners were much sought after.

There weren't, of course, the many alternative modes of viewing offered by today's cable, pay, and VCR technology. Remote-control devices, which make it virtually effortless to turn the television on or off or change channels, didn't exist. Instead, an awed and receptive audience sat in front of the screen, poised to watch. By 1954, when Clarence Birdseye's quick-freeze process had created a new market for frozen foods, advertisers also realized that an entirely new target audience was in place as well. A frozen prepackaged meal, complete with its own serving dish that could go in the oven and be ready to be served within forty-five minutes, was developed. It was called a "TV dinner."

From the beginning, television commercials have reflected society's mores and its technological capabilities. The earliest commercials utilized the "talking head" approach in which a spokesperson in the television studio talked to the camera, praising a specific product or even giving a rudimentary demonstration. When film and animation started being used for commercials, white-coated "doctors" provided narration while vignettes showed the benefits of over-the-counter medications, and "housewives" simulated the efficacious applications of various cleaning products. Today, Video Storyboard Tests, a research organization that monitors the impact of television commercials, identifies many different types, including:

- *Humor:* commercials that use humor to get the message across, such as the fast-talking spokesman for Federal Express's overnight delivery service, who promises that "absolutely, positively" the parcel will get where it's supposed to on time.
- *Children:* scenarios featuring likable and cute kids, among the most effective of this genre being Bill Cosby's Jell-O commercials.
- *Slice of life:* minidramas that simulate a real-life situation and show how using a certain product or service solves a problem, such as the Crest commercial in which a little girl can yell, "Look, Ma, no cavities," because her mother buys Crest toothpaste. Another example is MCI's takeoff on AT&T's effective emotional advertising; in the MCI spot, a mother is portrayed, weeping—not because her son told her that he loved her, via long distance, as he

does for AT&T, but because she has received a phone bill that the long-distance phone service MCI can substantially cut.

- *Musical or life-style:* commercials in which the product is shown in the context of events or activities with identifiable theme music appealing to viewer aspirations and emotions. This category includes most soft-drink spots, such as Pepsi-Cola's kids and teenagers playing on the beach accompanied by the music for "the Pepsi Generation."

- *Testimonials/expert endorsements:* commercials that use actors-as-experts or real experts to talk about a product or service. An example is the American Express "Do you know me?" campaign in which people with recognizable names but unfamiliar faces talk about carrying the American Express card whenever they travel.

- *Celebrities:* commercials in which well-known and recognizable personalities tout products.

- *Demonstrations:* commercials in which the use and efficacy of the product is shown or simulated, as when "ring around the collar" is removed by using Wisk as a laundry detergent.

- *Company presenter:* commercials in which the advertiser himself acts as spokesman, telling viewers about a product or service's virtues, such as Frank Perdue telling about his chicken's size and quality, and offering serving suggestions as well.

- *Presenter:* commercials in which a created character represents the product, as when Madge the manicurist shows how Palmolive Liquid can cure her customer's "dishwater hands" and Mr. Whipple extols Charmin's softness.

- *Animated cartoons:* commercials featuring characters such as Kellogg's "Tony the Tiger" for Frosted Flakes, or "Garfield the Cat" as the "spokescat" for Holiday Inn's subsidiary, Executive Suites.
- *Hidden-camera testimonials:* commercials that show ordinary consumers responding to the product without knowing that they are being filmed for a commercial.

Not only are there many different types of commercials today, but there are so many of them. In 1984, Video Storyboard Tests reported that the average person is exposed to about 2,400 commercials over a four-week period. This figure is undoubtedly increasing as sponsors air fifteen-second spots, instead of the previously common thirty-second ones. Advertisers obviously hope to create advertising that can break through all this commercial clutter and fulfill every advertiser's dream of creating a memorable, zap-proof spot in which the viewer's attention is held and his finger doesn't slide over to the remote-control button in order to see what's on another station.

Advertisers with money are producing a new commercial form, called the "blockbuster" or "breakthrough." Influenced by the popularity of MTV and music videos, these spots incorporate special visual and sound effects and use highly paid designers, technicians, celebrities, directors, stuntmen, and musicians. With production often costing over $1 million, these spots are events in themselves, promoted and publicized in much the same way as television specials.

European production, particularly that of Great Britain, has influenced American commercial production as well. Until recently, American directors did not have creative input into the commercials they filmed. Unlike their American counterparts, British commercial directors have long had creative involvement in advertising. Great Britain has been a leader in the production of visually striking, innovative advertising. During the late 1970s, the so-called British invasion took place and today a fair number of British directors are either working in the United States or are retained by American agencies who produce spots in England.

It is sometimes difficult for the viewer to realize that he is actually watching a commercial spot and not a music video when a "blockbuster" is aired. Most of these commercials combine visuals and music, with the voice-over, if any, just a tag line at the end. Many of these spots are specifically created to appeal to younger people, who, as Robert Pittman, former chief operating officer of MTV Networks, has said, "don't require a narrative line to take in information or entertainment [but] respond to more elusive sense impressions transferred by way of feelings, mood, and emotion."

Pepsi-Cola's "blockbuster" campaign in 1985 featured singer Lionel Richie singing the Pepsi message about "a whole new generation" with "new rhythms, new feelings and styles," and playing with a small child, visiting his grandmother, and working a crowd of his fans. These commercials made their debut as a three-minute paid spot over the Grammy Awards ceremony. Pepsi followed this, in 1986, with a two-minute spot in which "Miami Vice"'s Don Johnson and rock singer Glenn Frey wander into a high school dance to get help after their Ferrari breaks down. There was also a fantasy spot entitled "Earth," which was filmed in London by Ridley Scott. In it, a giant fissure opens in the parched earth of a Southwest American town; a Pepsi machine, spewing forth dozens of cans, is unearthed and a monumental thunderstorm unleashed.

Although such advertising extravaganzas might seem to

be attempting to attract a target audience primarily through entertainment, they are based upon research and carefully developed advertising strategy. After all, a client spending that type of money doesn't want a stunning but ineffective spot.

General Electric created its blockbuster, "The Power of Music," after research showed that most of the fourteen-to-twenty-four age segment that comprises the United States' largest market for tape decks, stereos, and radios perceived General Electric as a conservative, old-fashioned company when compared to its competition, Sony and Panasonic—yet, in blind-listening tests, invariably preferred the General Electric products. The company concluded that it had to change its image in the minds of this young target audience, and according to *ADWEEK*, allocated $65 million in national advertising to reach the "baby-boomers," one segment age fourteen to twenty-four and another eighteen to thirty-five.

Filmed in London and directed by Adrian Biddle, the director of photography on the film *Alien*, "The Power of Music" is a *Star Wars*-type fairy tale featuring a cast of over one hundred. Four interplanetary travelers arrive at a city in which there is total silence. Using their General Electric portable radios and tape players, the travelers break the silence, and the entire city begins to dance. The music wakes up a modern-day Sleeping Beauty, who falls in love with one of the heroes. The only voice-over in the spot is the tag line, "The power of music—no one lets you experience it like General Electric."

Sometimes a blockbuster is created only for limited but carefully selected appearance on national television. The Academy Awards, the Grammy Awards, and the Superbowl—now the nation's premiere (and most expensive, with a minute in 1986 costing $1.1 million) television event—act as showcases for carefully crafted, attention-getting, and expensive commercials. Apple Computer pioneered this with "1984," which it produced in order to announce the Macintosh computer. The spot made its debut over the 1984 Superbowl broadcast, garnering tremendous publicity and subsequent awards for its agency, Chiat/Day, and Apple Computer.

In 1985, Apple Computer decided to herald its entry into the business computer market with another blockbuster. Apple, the David to IBM's Goliath, developed a strategy in which Apple was to be presented as an alternative to IBM, with its reputation for conservatism and corporate blandness.

"Lemmings," as the new spot was named, took three fifteen-hour days to shoot, used 150 actors and a stunt team, and required location shots along the cliffs of Dover and in Sweden so that a specific type of cloud formation could be filmed. The spot showed a line of blindfolded businessmen and -women, singing a dirgelike rendition of the *Snow White and the Seven Dwarfs* song, "Hi ho, Hi ho, it's off to work we go," slowly shuffling forward in single file and falling off a cliff. The $600,000 spot was edited and plans were to broadcast it on the Superbowl time slot that Apple had purchased from ABC-TV at a cost of about $1 million.

However, when Apple's management saw the finished spot, they had grave doubts about using it. They believed the quality of the "Lemmings" spot didn't compare to "1984" and, even worse, might turn off the middle managers who were the very people Apple marketers had selected as the target for its advertising. Apple returned the time back to ABC-TV and decided not to run the spot.

By then, newspapers were running stories about "Lemmings" and the on-again, off-again plans to run it. Convinced by Chiat/Day, Apple repurchased the time for the last quarter of the game and decided to capitalize on the furor surrounding the spot by purchasing full-page ads in sixteen major newspapers throughout the nation that said, "If you go to the bathroom during the fourth quarter, you'll be sorry." Apple also arranged to have the commercial screened on the stadium's electronic scoreboard.

However, an SRI Research Center survey, which tests audience awareness of television advertising over a thirty-day period, showed that of the total number of respondents indicating that they had seen the spot, only 10.3 percent described it correctly. Almost 70 percent knew that they had seen an Apple commercial but didn't know what product the commercial was for. The spot simply failed to register with most viewers, and in the spring of 1986, Apple moved the account to BBDO, in part because of fallout from the "Lemmings" debacle but primarily because of management changes within the Apple organization. Apple stayed out of the Superbowl in 1986, giving IBM the unchallenged opportunity to air more than ten spots. As it turned out, the real star of the Superbowl was the Timex "Atlantis 100" spot. A sixty-second underwater fantasy with an eerie, understated sound track, the million-dollar-plus spot featured a ton-and-a-half watch model that was built in England, shipped to Israel, and then sunk fifty feet below the Red Sea with two tons of lead weight holding it down.

With all the logistics involved in shooting a spot for television, agencies use producers to coordinate all of the details of producing and completing commercials. Producers work with the casting, legal, account, creative, business-affairs, and talent-payment departments as well as the many outside suppliers that are involved in television production. Within the television production department are assistant producers and production assistants (the traditional entry-level position in the department). The casting department is also under the aegis of broadcast production.

During preproduction, producers prepare budgets, work with the casting department, and help select the director and production house. During production, the producer must handle any problems that arise and act as the liaison between agency and the production house that actually films the commercial. At postproduction, the producer follows the spot from its initial editing to the final copy that will go to television stations for broadcast.

Preproduction

Producers are part of the creative unit and work with the creative team, often at the beginning of concept development. Patty Wineapple, a producer at Grey Advertising, says: "Art directors and copywriters are creators. They aren't expected to have technical expertise. We are filmmakers. It's a good balance. We often get involved right after creative develops the concept or the initial storyboard. For instance, if a commercial is tested in animatic or scrapamatic [scrap material taken from magazines or newspapers and shot onto tape, in which form it can be screened before an audience] and it tests well, it might get budgeted out so we can see exactly what it will cost to produce. At that point, everyone may realize that the spot is just too expensive. I can often rework the concept and figure out how to produce it for less money. I know shortcuts. Sometimes there are ways of doing things technically that can save tremendous amounts of money. Say the art director has decided to do a package shot and is thinking of shooting it on a stage in a studio. That can be very expensive. We have to rent the studio and stage, light it, and hire a crew. Very often, the same thing can be accomplished using an animation stand [a table on which the object to be photographed stands where it is photographed by a special camera, frame by frame, to create an animated effect] in an optical house. Instead of spending forty thousand dollars for the effect, we may be able to do it for six thousand dollars."

Once the client gives the go-ahead to produce the spot, the agency hires a director. Television spots are rarely produced in-house at the agency. Instead, agencies retain a production house that specializes in commercial production. A production house is usually selected because a specific director either owns or works with the house. Typically, the agency chooses three directors and asks their production houses to bid on the job. Using either the six-page standard bid form prepared by the Association of Independent Commercial Producers or an agency's own form, the competing production houses itemize everything involved on a shoot, from salaries to projected film costs and telephone bills.

Producers know directors and understand which ones can best accomplish what is needed for the spot. Directors tend to specialize. Different directors are known for doing beauty, outdoors, animation, food, and slice-of-life. Says Wineapple: "I always ask the creative team if there are any directors who they particularly want to shoot the spot. We discuss certain types of directors and get reels sent over. Sometimes the art director will say 'I want to work with so-and-so; his work for a certain product was terrific.' I might say, 'I've worked with him and he's impossible. But director A does similar work and he's wonderful.'" Sometimes, for certain spots, usually blockbuster or particularly specialized ones, client and agency go directly to the director they want and negotiate a price. Most of the time, though, the director and production house are chosen on the basis of competitive bidding.

As mentioned before, the role of the director has changed in some instances. Certain directors are almost as well known as the products whose commercials they film. Until recently, the director was hired just to shoot the storyboard. He might occasionally have been asked for casting advice and he often helped choose the location. But the board was presented as a fait accompli. Once it was filmed, the agency took over postproduction, supervising the editing, music, and special effects. The director was, in reality, a skilled technician who was expected to put on film the action portrayed on the board and do it within set budgetary guidelines. Joe Sedelmaier, creator of Wendy's "Where's the beef?" commercials—in which he immortalized former manicurist Clara Peller registering outrage at the size of her puny burger—once said, "I never thought I'd go into commercials because of the lack of control."

Today certain directors call the shots, exercising that option from the development of the concept through final cut. These directors are hired precisely because the client and agency want that director's personal vision brought to the commercial spot.

In the United States, most of these directors began their careers working at advertising agencies. They understand that the goal of the spot is to sell the product. They are salesmen/filmmakers who know how a storyboard is developed and how best to get and hold the viewer's attention.

Of this group, the most popular among advertising professionals and known to the public through their work include: Bob Giraldi (Michael Jackson for Pepsi-Cola); Sid Meyers ("It's a good time for the great taste of McDonald's"); Joe Pytka (Pepsi's "Archaeology"); Steve Horn (Exxon's

"The spirit of America is the spirit of achievement"); Joe Sedelmaier (Wendy's "Where's the beef?"); and, from Great Britain, Ridley Scott (Apple's "1984" Macintosh spot) and his brother, Tony Scott (Apple's 1985 "Lemmings" spot).

Each of these directors has a unique style that is reflected by the look and feel of his commercial spots. They are also expensive. In a 1984 *ADWEEK* special issue, the magazine reported that a day's directing fee can cost between $7,500 and $13,000, plus a percentage if the commercial is brought in under budget. For example, if a commercial is budgeted at $100,000 and the director brings it in for $80,000, he gets a percentage of the $20,000 saved by client and agency. Depending upon the director's leverage, that percentage ranges from 10 to 35 percent.

Casting

While bids are being solicited from production houses, the producer, art director, and copywriter begin to work with the casting department in order to fill the roles in the commercial. Large agencies have full-time casting directors and smaller agencies can call on independent casting directors— over seventy operate in New York City alone. A "characterization study," describing the characters in the spot, is prepared. With the casting director, the creatives and the producer discuss the types of actors to be used. Working with the art director, copywriter, and agency producer, the casting director screens and auditions actors who might be right for the part.

Although most actors would probably prefer to work in film, television, or the theater, they are in a business with a very high unemployment rate and are usually ready and eager to work in commercials. According to the Screen Actors

Guild, television spots pay almost 50 percent of the fees that professional actors collect.

In order to keep track of new actors who might be good for commercials, casting directors attend many films and plays. They then contact agents who represent actors. When casting a role, the casting director is usually more concerned with an actor's look and style than with acting skill. A casting director who works for one of the largest agencies says of his work:

"Most of the time—ninety percent of the time—people don't have to act; it's the look that is crucial for a commercial. I once saw five hundred fifty people in order to cast four roles for a soft-drink commercial. It's different if you are casting someone to be a spokesperson. Then the person must have a presence and command—something that says 'listen to me' but isn't threatening. It's hard to find someone who can do that for thirty seconds and sell the product. But usually we are looking for a certain kind of face. A husband who sits at the breakfast table while the wife has all the dialogue and whose only move is to take a spoon in his hand and say, 'Yum' doesn't require brilliant acting. It requires a look that goes with the wife.

"I always think about the commercial as an entire entity. When I am casting a group, I cast the pivotal character first. If it's a family, that is usually the woman. I then build the family around her. Little things like making sure that the husband and kids match one another in hair and eye color and that the overall family look is the same are very important because you never know how the commercial will end up. Even though the husband may not have had a single word to say and is merely an onlooker, in the final cut he may appear on every single frame."

If a celebrity is to be used, the casting director makes the initial contact. He calls the celebrity's agent to find out whether the celebrity is willing to do a commercial and what fees and other conditions are required.

Celebrities can be a mixed blessing. Most consider it beneath them to audition for a commercial spot. Not all can sell like a Bill Cosby, who has spoken so effectively for Jell-O and Coke, or a Mean Joe Green, whose Coke commercial, according to a 1984 *New York* magazine column, still had the highest recall score of any other spot. Sometimes a performer who comes off magnificently in a film or television series is a bomb at pitching products. Sometimes the celebrity is ridiculed for undertaking a commercial endorsement, and the whole idea backfires. After former presidential candidate Geraldine Ferraro accepted $75,000 for a Diet-Pepsi spot in which she appeared with her two daughters—telling them that as part of "a new generation . . . you can be anything you want to be"— she seemed to spend more time on television defending her decision to appear in the commercial than actually being seen in it.

Even dead celebrities can be expensive. Advertisers must get rights from the estate, which according to the *New York Times*, can cost up to $10,000 for one use in a sixty-second spot. The estate of Louis Armstrong received a five-figure payment for a split-second image of the trumpeter in a TV spot. Elvis Presley, Buddy Holly, Laurel and Hardy, and Charlie Chaplin (as the "Little Tramp") are among celebrities whose photographs or representations have recently been used by companies including IBM, Toyota, and Anheuser-Busch.

There is a danger, as well, that the use of a famous person may detract from the commercial's effect. Although the celebrity registers audience recognition, it doesn't necessarily mean that the television viewer is paying attention to the commercial message. He may just be noticing the celebrity. It is important that the celebrity somehow be linked or personally connected with the product being pushed. When Lynn Redgrave acted as spokesperson for Weight Watchers, even though she performed a script prepared by Doyle Dane Bernbach copywriters, she was telling her own story—and the believability translated onto the screen. On the other hand, when Pillsbury and its agency Leo Burnett produced a commercial to promote the company's new Crusty French Loaf using an Inspector Clouseau look-alike as spokesman, research showed that viewers remembered Inspector Clouseau more than the bread. Pillsbury revised the spot, giving the product more air time and stressing the brand name.

Sometimes the client becomes the star of the commercial. Lee Iacocca speaks for Chrysler, Frank Borman for Eastern Airlines, Frank Perdue for his chickens. They became celebrities because of their widely seen appearances on behalf of their products. The presenter's personality is certainly important in determining the spot's success, but the type of business also seems to make a difference. Research has shown that people like to see chief operating officers in ads for restaurants, banks, automobiles, stock brokerage houses, and airlines. They are not interested in seeing the owners of oil, chemical, beer, or tobacco companies.

There is always the possibility that something might happen in the celebrity's life to undermine his or her effectiveness as a commercial presenter. Although it doesn't happen very often, a celebrity who is involved in a scandal can cause a great deal of embarrassment for the client. In 1973, Procter & Gamble quickly changed the picture on its Ivory Snow boxes when Marilyn Chambers, who had been photographed cuddling a baby on the package, turned out to be the star of the pornographic movie, *Behind the Green Door*. Almost a decade later, Vanessa Williams was forced to renounce her Miss America title—and, in the process, give up several lucrative advertising contracts—when *Penthouse* magazine published compromising photographs taken before the Miss America pageant. Not to lose any opportunity for its own self-promotion, the Ingels Agency, which represents many celebrities for commercial ventures, decided to advertise its services with the line, "If you want a celebrity and you're weary of the hassle."

Casting decisions are not easily made. One copywriter says that casting seems to cause worse arguments than any other part of the advertising process. Creatives have strong opinions about which people will best take the words and actions portrayed on the storyboard and bring them to life on film. Account people tend to become very protective of what they perceive to be client feelings; and, of course, the clients themselves frequently have strong opinions.

Once budgets are set, casting is in place, and the production house has been chosen, there is a preproduction meeting that is attended by everybody involved in the commercial. The client, agency producers, account, and creative are there, along with everybody from the production house that has been chosen to film the spot. Every detail is discussed, including set, location, wardrobe, music, and talent. The director explains how the spot is going to be filmed and goes over the projected timetable. This is the time during which last-minute concerns and problems will hopefully be taken care of, because once production is under way, changes will be difficult and expensive.

Production

The day of the shoot can be tense. If it is the first campaign for a new product or one that is being repositioned, the shoot is often the culmination of years of work. All of the efforts—account, research, creative—will now be focused on the creation of a sixty-, thirty-, or fifteen-second piece of film or tape.

The client wants to be sure that the product looks good and translates well onto film. The account person is concerned about the client. The copywriter is thinking about the words and their nuances. The art director is looking at the set, props, and the costumes that have been arranged by the stylist. Everybody is focused on the director. But the producer is ultimately responsible for making sure that the spot that has been approved by the client is filmed on time and on budget.

"The shoot is the day of reckoning," says producer Patty Wineapple. "If all the preproduction work is done with care, on the actual day of the shoot there is little for us to do except make sure that what we have actually promised gets done. The production house really takes over that day. I am the liaison between the agency and the production house. For a director who is trying to direct talent and crew to have to listen to clients, art directors, and copywriters and cope with six other people yelling in his ear is impossible. It is much more orderly if things go through one person."

It is important that everybody reach a consensus on what the spot is to achieve and how it must be done. The creative team knows how the commercial should appear, and the producer is there to make that happen. Art directors and copywriters do often get involved during production. As Marty Muller says: "By reading something with a certain inflection, the entire meaning of a line can be changed. The writer sometimes has to oversee the director. The director can bring the talent out of the actor, but the writer knows what she wants to hear. The writer often has to jump in and say,

'This is what it is supposed to be.'" But a strong producer is the link between agency and production house and can prevent such expensive but not uncommon occurrences as twenty takes for one line, last-minute lighting and costume changes, and, as one art director recalled, "Three people from the client choosing the hamburger buns to be photographed, and literally counting to see which ones had the most sesame seeds on top."

Postproduction

All commercials used to be filmed. But today many are taped. Tape is less expensive than film because revisions during postproduction are much easier, essentially all part of a one-step process. In addition, all television programming, including commercials, is broadcast from tape. So even a spot that has been shot and edited on film must be transferred to tape for television broadcast.

The most selective directors still almost always use film because it has a softer, more realistic look than tape. But, in the past few years, tape quality has improved dramatically. If the lighting is good and the spot has been shot correctly, most people can't tell the difference between a filmed spot and a taped spot.

At the end of each day's shoot, everybody views the dailies, or "rushes," which consist of every bit of film or tape shot during the session. When production is completed, if the spot has been taped, editing begins right at the tape house with the agency producer and art director working with a tape editor who programs instructions into computerized equipment. Often the other members of the creative team are present as well. If the spot is on film, a film editor works with the producer and agency creatives to prepare a rough cut. As they go frame by frame, the final fifteen-, thirty-, or sixty-second spot is created from hours of film.

Clients usually see the rough cut and approve it, and sometimes the director does as well. Most of the time, though, the director's job stops with the shoot. One producer says: "A director who wants the spot for his reel or is very close to the agency will come. But usually, he's not involved. The money stops coming in after the shoot."

Tape houses vary in quality; the best have millions of dollars' worth of computerized equipment that can accomplish in seconds what it used to take highly specialized film services days to achieve. For instance, if the spot is going to be edited on film, it goes to an optical house, at which all special visual effects will be added. Perhaps there will be special titles, an animated figure moving across the screen, or a picture of the product in center screen with a product spokesman appearing in a small box in the upper-right-hand corner. On film, all of this is done in an optical house. However, if the edit is on tape, a tape house can do everything that an optical house can do and usually more quickly. The tape editor simply gives the computer instructions, the image is put on the screen, and, if everyone approves, it is incorporated into the final tape.

Most tape houses have equipment that can create special effects and solve technical problems immediately, although at extra cost. For instance, an ADO (Ampex Digital Optics), which costs about $300 an hour, can take a picture and flip it, make it into quadrants, enlarge it or reduce it. A *mirage*, at about $450 an hour, can curl a picture all the way up and off the screen or break a picture up into pieces and put it back together. For $80 an hour, a *character generator* changes the "super"—any graphic material that appears over the commercial.

Although dialogue is recorded at the shoot, music and voice-over are added during final postproduction. A final mix puts the visual and audio elements together onto a master copy that will be duplicated and forwarded by the traffic department to the stations over which the commercial is to be aired.

MUSIC

Music is as important as words and visuals in advertising today. Indeed, music is frequently the key element in establishing mood and transmitting the commercial message. It is considered so important a part of advertising that the large agencies have music departments staffed by music producers. Smaller agencies can call on the services of independent music producers.

Technology has made music pervasive. There are music videos, MTV, electronic amplification, and portable and inexpensive radios and tape decks with audio quality better than that of the most expensive and sophisticated equipment two decades ago. Portability has made music part of daily routine rather than something chosen for special times or events. Advertisers understand that the choice of music plays a key role in getting the target audience's attention. According to the *Wall Street Journal*, music is considered so important in marketing, particularly to teens, that Coca-Cola studies the lyrics of the top twenty singles each week to see what kinds of common themes and moods are expressed.

As advertising continues to expand globally, music becomes even more important; it is universal and can transcend cultural differences. The popular music of the United States and Great Britain is as well known internationally as in its own countries. With unified advertising extending across national boundaries, music is often substituted for words.

Music producers are trained musicians who work with the creative team, helping them decide on the music that best expresses the commercial message. Music producers handle royalties, licensing fees, and production and studio budgets. Like the television producer, the music producer is responsible for making sure that the music part of the commercial is done on time and within budget.

Just as the producer works with an outside production house and director, the music producer works with outside music suppliers that service the advertising business. Music producers also arrange for sound effects and stock music, which are purchased from music libraries and sound-effects suppliers. Music producers retain contractors who hire musicians for recording sessions, singers, arrangers, and orchestrators. They arrange for recording- and mixing-studio space.

Music producers also contract for original music. There are composers who write music specifically for commercials. Some work alone but many own or work for what are called "jingle houses." Sometimes the copywriter writes the words and a composer puts the jingle—the musical equivalent of advertising copy—to music. More often, though, the copywriter has a rough idea for a jingle and a composer creates the final version. Jingles such as Sid Woloshin's work for McDonald's ("You deserve a break today" and "You, you're the one") and for Pan American World Airways ("Pan Am makes the going great") are lasting examples of the advertising promise set into the lyric.

The music producer gets involved at the very beginning of commercial production in order to help the creative team decide what type of music should be used. Hunter Murtaugh, head of the music department at Young & Rubicam, says, "We look at the advertising, evaluate it, and make musical suggestions. We want the music and advertising integrated in such a way that it is entertaining but will also sell the product. Often the copywriter and art director have an idea about what they want the music to accomplish but don't know how to do it. I can speak to them about the advertising concept and put it into a musical context."

Together, creative and the music producer decide at what point during production music should be selected or written. Sometimes the decision is made after the spot is filmed. For instance, the spot might need a musical score to highlight its emotional component, as in most Hallmark or AT&T commercials. In that case, everybody waits for a finished spot before deciding on what music to purchase or the type of original music to commission.

"Sometimes," says Murtaugh, "the music is the skeleton of the commercial. We choose the music and create the spot around it. The Oil of Olay spot that uses the Roberta Flack song, 'The First Time Ever I Saw Your Face,' was created around the song."

Often, the music and lyric themselves express the advertising strategy, and an entire campaign is planned around a particular musical theme. The various pool-outs will use different arrangements and executions of the same theme. The music establishes the brand personality, becoming, as Murtaugh says, "the anthem for the product."

In 1982, the Dr Pepper Company decided to reposition its soft drink. It had been unsuccessfully competing with the mass-appeal Coca-Cola and Pepsi-Cola using its "Be a Pepper" theme. Dr Pepper managers and its agency, Young & Rubicam, commissioned psychographic research to identify and describe soft-drink users. Using the Values and Life-style Program (VALS), which places consumers into pre-defined categories, Dr Pepper and the Young & Rubicam agency discovered that 50 percent of all soft-drink customers between the ages of eighteen and twenty-five fell into the "Inner-Directed" category, perceiving themselves as independent and not easily influenced by others (figures from *ADWEEK*).

The Dr Pepper Company and Young & Rubicam decided to reposition the soft drink and direct its advertising toward that "Inner-Directed" audience. In 1984, the agency produced seven commercials, each created around the jingle, "Hold out, hold out, for the out-of-the-ordinary Dr Pepper." The $35 million campaign emphasized the target audience's individualism by having such characters as Godzilla and a Quasimodo-type hunchback refuse offers of any drink except Dr Pepper.

Once the music is selected or recorded, the music producer acts as liaison between the creative team and the composer or orchestrator. "For instance," says Murtaugh, "the copywriter might say that a particular piece of music sounds 'too airy' or 'light.' I can turn that statement into a musical expression so that the composer understands just what that means. We know the language and the technique that is used when music is created. It's like using correct grammar."

There are trends in the kind of music used for commercials. As Murtaugh says: "Commercials are like life in the fast lane. Remember, we are dealing only in sixty-, thirty-, and now fifteen-second increments. We are trying to provide emotional feelings in that time period. Styles change so frequently and quickly. You never know what's going to last."

During the mid-1980s, popular music of the sixties became popular again. The target audience for many advertisers are the same people who were raised on this music.

According to *Advertising Age,* advertisers pay up to $200,000, as opposed to the $10,000 to $25,000 charged for a piece of original music, to purchase the rights to sixties hits, even hiring name performers of the sixties to perform in these musical commercials. Dr. John and Richie Havens, the same men who brought acres of people to their feet at Woodstock almost twenty years ago, are today singing "Come on, baby, let the ScotTowels roll," "Because time goes by" (for Kodak), and plugging McDonald's. Chuck Berry even adapted the rock 'n' roll classic, "No Particular Place to Go," for Volkswagen.

Murtaugh was involved in what has been called "the *Big Chill* commercial" for Lincoln-Mercury. Created to appeal to consumers who prefer foreign cars and associate large American cars both with overconsumption and their parents' generation, it used the John Lennon/Paul McCartney song, "Help," with the rights reportedly costing $100,000. The ad synchronized the lyrics with visuals showing the advantages of driving a Mercury. For instance, to show how the Mercury stays in control and drives easily, five Mercuries speed in perfect synchronization around a maypole to the words, "I do appreciate your being 'round."

Murtaugh says, "The people of the sixties are grown up. They have money, jobs, and new consumer needs. Ads have to reach them. To connect the car with the consumer, the music takes them back to when they learned how to drive and what cars meant to them. Everyone who drives has slammed the door to a car, put his foot on the gas, and felt free.

"The thing that people remember first—the thing that makes them look—is the sound. It's the emotional connector between you and the picture. TV is very boring without the sound on. When you look at a piece of film, if you put different kinds of music to it, the mood changes. That's why we adapt the music to the market we are trying to reach."

PRINT PRODUCTION

The print-production department is where print advertising is prepared for placement in print media. The amount of actual production done in-house varies from agency to agency, with many using outside suppliers for all the steps in print preparation, and others maintaining agency art studios in which some production is done.

When the art director and copywriter develop an advertising concept or idea, it is usually presented to senior creatives in the form of a layout, which gives a rough idea of what the ad will look like. A layout is a rough sketch with a hand-lettered headline. When creative and account are ready to present the ad to the client for approval, this rough layout is presented as a comprehensive layout, or "comp," which is a more accurate representation of the advertising idea. In smaller agencies, the art director often does layouts. Larger agencies have layout artists who work in the bull pen preparing layouts under the supervision of the art director. However, many art directors choose to do these initial layouts themselves.

Once the ad is approved by the client, it goes into production. The first step in this process is to prepare a paste-up or a mechanical, consisting of type proofs and artwork, which provides an accurate representation of the finished ad. The actual advertising material is prepared by an outside photo platemaker or color separator. The production manager must understand the process of color separation, offset—as opposed to rotogravure printing—and every other facet of production. He is responsible for making sure that the colors that will be reproduced in the final ad are accurate. A cosmetic ad showing a new lipstick color, for instance, must accurately represent the true shade of the product.

All agencies have print-production departments, although the number of support personnel varies greatly from agency to agency. In some agencies, art directors manage almost all details of print production; in others, the production department takes over, carrying out the creative decisions made by the art director. Typically, the print-production department is composed of: production managers, who are in charge of overseeing the quality of all artwork produced for the agency; art buyers, who purchase the material or services that will be used to make up the ad; type directors, who help select typeface; and proofreaders, who are responsible for checking finished ads.

The art buyer is typically the first person to begin working on production. According to Donald H. Insull, head of print production at William Esty, the function of art buyer is a relatively new one, in existence for about five years and still restricted pretty much to the larger agencies. The art buyer might be compared to the television producer, functioning, says Insull, "as the business part of the art director." The art buyer helps the art director select a photographer or illustrator in much the same way the television producer works with the art director and copywriter in selecting a director.

"This," says art director Gerry O'Hara, "is a crucial choice, as the final look of the ad is very much a product of the photographer's style and sensibility." Some photographers specialize in fashion, portraits, food, or outdoor, or are known for their proficiency in handling technical details, which is important if the ad is to incorporate special effects.

Although most art directors themselves know the work of photographers and ultimately make the selection, the art buyer works out all the logistics, for instance, scheduling the shoot, setting up casting sessions with the casting department if necessary, and making sure that models sign releases. In addition, the art buyer estimates costs and prepares purchase orders.

At the same time that the art director or art buyer are working on production details, the type director is working with creative to determine the actual type to be used on the headline and copy. There are more than five thousand different type styles from which to choose. Says O'Hara, "It's important to choose a type that will give the ad some personality or strongly communicate what it is you are saying in the ad." Although some agencies have typesetting departments, most use outside suppliers. The type director prepares type estimates and helps select the best type shop for the project, supervising its work and checking for accuracy.

The overall responsibility for production is assumed by a production manager. When the ad is finished, each publication in which it will appear must receive its own copy. Print production is highly technical and becoming more so each day. For those interested in the details of print production, the International Paper Company publishes an annual guide to production called *Pocket Pal* (available from Pocket Pal Books, P.O. Box 100, Church Street Station, New York, New York 10016).

JOBS

Print production and broadcast production are two distinct departments within agencies. Positions in broadcast production are probably the most difficult ones in advertising to get. Although a knowledge of film and television production is helpful, it won't get you the job. Basically, aspiring producers begin as gofers and work their way up to assistant producer or production assistant, where they handle clerical details and assist the producer. Unlike other creative jobs, where prospective employers can see something tangible in the form of the portfolio, this isn't true for production. It's a question of getting one's foot in the door and then by hard work and good performance moving up the ladder.

Print is not as difficult to break into. Print-production managers can begin as assistants in the production department or as proofreaders, or move from the print traffic department. Most have training or experience in visual and graphic arts and some background in typography, design, and layout. Starting salaries in broadcast and print production vary widely depending upon experience, region, and level of entry. However, both print and broadcast beginners start with annual salaries of between $13,000 and $15,000.

8

Traffic

With so much going on at once in so many different departments, it is obvious that there is a real potential for chaos within agencies. Somebody has got to be responsible for the work flow from the time the agency gets the go-ahead from the client to begin creative work until that work is completed and, in finished form, sent to the media in which it will appear. The aptly named traffic department handles this. All agencies have someone in charge of traffic, and large agencies usually have separate departments for print and broadcast traffic.

The structure of the traffic department varies from agency to agency. In some, traffic is a separate department, often working under the aegis of the print-production and broadcast-operations departments or sometimes even the media department. In others, traffic is part of the account department, and traffic coordinators work with account reps on specific pieces of business.

Work on a piece of advertising officially begins when the account department issues a job order that lists all pertinent information about the piece of work that is going into production. The job order is then assigned a job number, which is a permanent billing code under which all work is billed. The print traffic department often oversees production, whereas broadcast traffic doesn't ordinarily assume this role. The agency's creative team works closely with the outside suppliers who produce broadcast material. However, the broadcast traffic department is in charge of disseminating the finished ads to the proper media and tries to insure that production remains on schedule. If the order is for print, traffic gets a list from the media department of all publications in which the advertising is going to appear and then determines actual production needs. Each publication has its own requirements; traffic orders the ads, making sure they are produced in correct quantity, size, and color, and for either an offset or rotogravure printing process.

In addition to production details, traffic is responsible for scheduling the work. Traffic ascertains publication closing dates and then works backward to determine creative and production deadlines. In many agencies, a lot of this is coordinated by computers, such as William Esty's critical path analysis (CPA) computer program. By putting into the computer a publication's closing date and information about a particular job's production details, the computer can tell at what point each step must be begun in order to make the closing deadline.

Both print and broadcast traffic departments are responsible for getting advertising to the right place at the right time and with the correct scheduling instructions. In a large agency, this might involve sending over two million commercial spots a year to network and local television and radio stations and even more print ads. This is not so difficult when a single spot is to be aired as part of a network show or an ad is to run in a monthly national publication. Most network programs are pretaped and prerecorded. Commercials are integrated into the programs a week or two before air date. And in the case of a monthly magazine, traffic makes sure that the advertising material arrives by the closing date.

However, the traffic function is usually not so simple. For example, both print and broadcast traffic handle special advertising for test markets and specific localities. One traffic manager, talking about broadcast, says, "Sometimes test commercials are running in certain areas. Say a package-goods account is running a toothpaste commercial over a network Monday-night movie. At the same time, it is copy testing new commercials for that same toothpaste in certain areas of the country. We have to arrange for the test commercial to be aired in those markets at the same time the national spot is being aired in all others. This is called a cut-in. If the cut-in gets messed up, we have a disaster, because all the research can be knocked off." This is particularly complicated because network television shows don't originate from one location but from several locations throughout the country.

Print media presents the same complications, and frequently both offset and rotogravure ads must be prepared for the same publication. If a product is being tested in one market, it may require a special ad; as part of a limited run, an ad may very well be printed offset instead of using the more economical rotogravure process usually used by national publications that print millions of copies. It is a traffic department task, and it is the traffic manager's responsibility to make sure that the right ad, correctly produced, gets to the proper location in time for the publication's closing date.

Speaking about the traffic position, Nancy Bruya, head of broadcast traffic at Grey Advertising, says: "Generally speaking, traffic people work under a great deal of stress. Everything seems to happen at the last minute or at five P.M. on Friday. You are working with account, media, and creative people who are often under stress themselves. You must be able to work with people. But for a person who is detail-oriented and likes the opportunity to deal with people in the various departments, this can be a rewarding job. Don't forget: you can have the best creative and media plan in the world, but if it doesn't get on the air, it's for naught."

Because traffic involves contact with practically every agency function, the traffic department is often seen as a stepping-stone to the account or media departments. This is more true in small agencies than in large, urban-based agencies, although it is not unusual for people to move from traffic into broadcast operations, spot buying, or print production. Within large agencies, print traffic appears to offer more opportunities for upward mobility than broadcast, probably because print traffic people are very much involved in actual production as well as scheduling and distribution, whereas in broadcast, producers handle production.

Although a college degree isn't a prerequisite for employment in the traffic department, with a degree it is sometimes possible to bypass the entry-level assistant traffic position and become a traffic coordinator. The average starting salary is about $13,500.

9

Broadcast Administration

With so many administrative and financial details involved in television production, many agencies have broadcast-administration departments. At a small agency, the producer may very well handle everything with assistance from the agency's traffic and business personnel. But a large agency has business managers—or broadcast coordinators, as they are frequently called—who monitor production finances and costs, and talent-payment personnel who handle the complex fees paid to actors who appear in the commercials.

Although these positions are in broadcast, they are not stepping-stones to producing jobs. Rather, they require facility with detail, record keeping, and accounting skills. These positions are becoming increasingly important as broadcast production costs continue to rise and clients insist on strict accountability from their agencies. According to the Association of National Advertisers, in 1985 the average cost of producing a spot in New York City was $200,000. And the average cost of purchasing thirty seconds over prime time was, according to the A. C. Nielsen Company, almost $95,000—practically triple the cost ten years ago. In addition, with almost $60 million a year spent on commercials that for one reason or another don't work and are never even broadcast, clients are concerned about keeping costs down, adhering to the budget, and making sure that the planned commercial is effective once it is produced.

Business managers get involved with the commercial at the start of preproduction. They help cost out (estimate the cost of producing) storyboards and set realistic budgets for commercials. They understand all of the hidden costs that might make a commercial go over budget and often try to ascertain whether potentially expensive details of the commercial are really necessary. If a spot uses an animal, for instance, liability insurance must be purchased; but if the animal is under six months old, insurance isn't required. The business manager might ask whether a puppy would do as well as a dog. Or, if the spot is going to be shot at an outdoor location, the business manager points out that it could rain for five days, and makes sure that the client is willing to absorb the costs involved in such a delay.

Business managers examine and keep track of all the bids submitted by production houses. They work with the agency producer developing specifications ("specs") for all aspects of production and with the production houses to make sure that the submitted bids include these specs. With producers, business managers work up talent-payment estimates for production sessions, reviewing final contracts sent to them by the casting department to compare estimated payments with actual contracted payments. Says Nancy Kessler, head of the business-affairs department at Grey Advertising, "A lot of the time you think you are paying someone scale and when you see the contract, it turns out that special provisions have been added and you are paying extra money."

While the spot is being filmed, business affairs monitors production, making sure that contracts are followed, costs are consistent with the accepted bid, and overages are approved. When the spot is complete, the business manager screens it. Nancy Kessler explains, "We look to see if everyone who was hired as an on-camera principal is still there. Must any actor be upgraded from extra to principal? Did the producer remember to tell us that there is music? We might find that three people who were hired as principals aren't principals anymore. That saves money."

The production house pays for most production details, including the crew, script supervisor, stylist, designers, builders, makeup artists, home economists for food shots, and, if children or animals are involved, nurses or animal trainers. These expenses are all covered in the bid submitted by the production house. But the agency pays the actors. Once the commercial is completed, although actors have been paid session fees for their time while filming the spot, they later begin to receive residual payments whenever the spot is aired. This is the job of talent payment.

Actors who appear in commercials are members of the Screen Actors Guild and work under the SAG Commercial Contract, a document over seventy pages long that covers every item of employment and compensation. It is a very complex document. Even Nancy Kessler, who is part of the negotiating committee on which agency and union representatives sit when negotiating new contracts, says, "When someone asks me a question about the SAG contract, I have to look it up and think twice."

The contract defines such work-related items as exactly

what qualifies as a principal role and where it should apply; special children's rules; night-work, holiday, and weekend regulations; travel time and distance provisions; meal schedules; and overtime rules. It also contains the rules upon which residual payments to actors are based. At a large agency with a lot of commercial production, millions of dollars are paid out each year to commercial talent.

Talent payment is not simply a question of signing a check. It is incredibly complicated, with details that could confuse the most organized and alert of individuals. The amount of a residual to be paid, for example, depends on whether the commercial is network, local, or cable, and on how many and in what cities it is broadcast. There are also categories within these basic distinctions: If the commercial is broadcast over a local station during a station break and not connected to a specific program, it is called a "wild spot." If, at the beginning of a show, the spot advertises one of the sponsor's products and that product does not appear again, it is a "cow catcher." Another spot that advertises a second product of the sponsor and is broadcast following the show is called a "hitchhike." In each case, the residual payment amount is different.

All commercial production operates in the context of thirteen-week cycles. When an actor appears in a commercial, the first day of work becomes the first day of a thirteen-week fixed cycle. The fee received for the day's employment is called a session fee, which also gives the client the right to use that commercial for thirteen weeks and prevents the actor from doing spots for competitive products for the same length of time.

To keep the commercial viable and to "hold" the actor, the actor is paid an additional holding fee every thirteen weeks. This is often done even if the client decides not to use the spot during a given thirteen-week cycle. Certain products are seasonal. If General Foods produces a spot for Kool-Aid and the spot works well, General Foods may very well decide to use the same spot the following summer. The actors appearing in the spot are paid holding fees for the fixed thirteen-week cycles throughout the fall, winter, and spring even though the spot isn't being aired. Sometimes clients pay holding fees as insurance. Perhaps a new commercial is in production and it turns out not to work (remember that $60 million spent on commercials that never run). If the client paid holding fees, he can use the old spot.

Although these jobs in broadcast administration are not glamour jobs, they are important. Says Kessler, "You must be strong. You can be treated like a bookkeeper if you are not careful. Producers are glitzy: they are the stars here. We sit at the desks and they run around and speak to the actors. But we are the people who are ultimately responsible for the client's money."

10

Commercial Clearance

Hype, hucksterism, charlatanism—all these terms have been used to describe advertising. And since truth in advertising has at times been elusive, advertising in the United States today is a highly regulated business.

As early as 1872, postal-fraud laws prohibited the use of the mail to defraud. In 1906 the Pure Food and Drug Act was passed in response to self-proclaimed healers who promoted patent medicines and home remedies of dubious value. In 1914 the Federal Trade Commission was established to monitor unfair business practices and in 1938 the FTC was granted additional powers by Congress, giving it the authority to seek court injunctions in cases of potentially dangerous advertisements for foods, drugs, and cosmetics.

Today the Federal Trade Commission (FTC), the Food and Drug Administration, the U.S. Postal Service, the Securities and Exchange Commission, the Federal Deposit Insurance Corporation, the Federal Home Loan Bank Board, the Federal Reserve Board, the Treasury Department Bureau of Alcohol, Tobacco, and Firearms, and the Civil Aeronautics board all have powers to act in cases of false or misleading advertising. In addition to these federal agencies, most states regulate advertising as well.

It is the FTC that has the most power. In the 1970s, it forced Campbell's Soup and its agency BBDO to stop using marbles beneath the vegetables in vegetable-soup photographs to make it appear as if there were a lot more vegetables than there really were. It later ordered Listerine, at a cost of $10 million, to run corrective advertising after the mouthwash maker claimed that using its product would help prevent sore throats and colds.

In addition to the supervision of government organizations, the advertising industry polices itself by supporting the self-regulatory National Advertising Review Board and the National Advertising Division of the Better Business Bureau.

These regulatory organizations initiate action either on their own or in response to complaints from consumers or competitors after a commercial has appeared. Under the Reagan administration, the FTC is not as active as it has been in the past. As a result, there are increasing numbers of cases in which competitors sue one another through the judicial system over deceptive advertising claims. A case in point is the highly publicized conflict between Hertz and Avis over Hertz's claim, made in the spring of 1984, that it had more *new* cars than Avis had. Avis sued and won, showing that Hertz had 97,000 1984 cars when it made its claim but that Avis actually had a total fleet of 102,000. Hertz was ordered to publish corrective advertising in six publications.

In order to avoid the time and money that must be spent defending a challenge, to say nothing of the negative publicity that follows, agencies review advertising material before it appears. Internal review procedures try to insure that all claims can be substantiated and that the advertising is truthful and accurate. Some of the larger agencies have lawyers on staff, but all retain lawyers who, in addition to handling the numerous licensing and contractual matters between the agency and its clients, suppliers, talent, and networks, advise on whether advertising is legally sound.

This is most important in the case of television. No client or agency wants to spend money producing a television spot and discover that it cannot be used. With television, not only must federal regulations be followed but in addition, each network has its own guidelines regarding taste and acceptability. Before a television commercial can be aired, television networks and stations must approve the spot. This is called commercial clearance. Large agencies that produce hundreds of commercials each year often have people who work full time with network commercial-clearance departments getting the agency's advertising approved. If an agency schedules a commercial that has not been formally cleared for broadcast, it must pay a fine.

Creatives are sensitive to the potential problems of commercial clearance and often check before putting ideas to paper. Dick Walburger, one of two staff lawyers at DFS/ Dorland, says, "Creative calls all the time. For instance, I recently had an inquiry from a group supervisor who wanted to know if using the word 'hell' would be a problem. The creative group had a cute idea that involved using the word in the context of a 'hellish day' for a man under a lot of pressure. They wanted to show a hot environment and it was for a product that really related to that.

"I had to say, 'I hate to tell you this, but you'll never get it on the air.' The advertising agency has one product and that is the advertising it produces. If advertising is produced that cannot be aired or is challenged by a federal agency or private-sector lawsuit by a consumer or competitor, it just diverts our resources to counterproductive areas."

The process of commercial clearance begins when the storyboard is approved. In some agencies, the account-services department sends the storyboard to the network on which the spot will run. When approval is given, production begins. Other agencies are more cautious and have instituted procedures under which both client and agency legal staffs check the storyboard as well. In agencies with commercial-clearance personnel, the storyboard is given a preliminary review before it is sent on to the legal staff and network commercial-clearance departments.

The storyboard with accompanying script is checked to make sure that no trade regulations are violated and that the advertising is not false, misleading, deceptive, or ambiguous. If a claim is made, it must be substantiated. Usually supporting information is submitted by the client's research and development department.

Loretta Donato, director of legal clearance at Grey Advertising, says, "I look for the basic things from both a legal and a network clearance perspective. Are there posters on the wall for the National Football League; are the kids wearing Little League uniforms? If so, do we have permission? Do we have rights to the music that is being used? Is money or the flag shown? You can't do that. What about words like 'new,' 'free,' 'warranty,' 'guarantee'? I want to know exactly what they mean. Is there a contest? If so, we examine every detail. Is the ad in good taste? Are there any implicit or overt claims? If so, we need substantiation and ask the account group to get the support from the client."

After the networks have completed their review, the storyboard is returned with comments concerning claims, net impression, and taste. There are special regulations and conditions affecting commercials directed toward children.

These regulations were instituted in response to commercials such as the Mattel Toy's spot introducing Hot Wheels. Filmed in slow motion and speeded up in postproduction, the commercial showed the cars going at breakneck speed, perhaps 150 mph. Children watching the spot had no idea what the cars were really like.

"A network," says Donato, "might look at a storyboard that shows a child sliding down a banister and say that it isn't safe. We respond by adding a parent to the situation so that it is obvious someone will catch the child if he falls. Networks are also concerned about overglamorizing commercials directed toward children. Sometimes we have to change furniture because the initial storyboard might have portrayed something too elaborate and upscale, not representative of most children's rooms.

"You can't be exhortative to children. For instance, you aren't permitted to say something costs 'only a quarter.' And under no circumstances can an advertisement encourage a child to ask a parent to buy something. If the commercial shows toys, it must not exaggerate their size or performance."

Commercial clearance is often a time-consuming process during which network and agency negotiate and compromises are reached. Networks tend to be cautious, even questioning puffery, which is a statement of obvious exaggeration. A commercial might contain copy that says "it tastes like sunshine" or "the most beautiful thing in the world." Obviously, no one could possibly substantiate such claims, and agencies find this type of challenge frustrating.

In these kinds of situations, agencies with full-time, experienced clearance personnel have an advantage over those agencies in which the account personnel handle clearance for their clients. Over time, those who coordinate network clearance for all agency accounts know what the networks have or have not allowed in the past and usually have long-term working relationships with their network counterparts. Through practice, they have finely honed their negotiating skills as well. Regardless of experience, however, when an objective claim is made—for instance, that brand A is twenty times more powerful than brand B—it had better be provable.

Taste is another frequent area of conflict between networks and agency. Rosemary Nelson, a lawyer at Young & Rubicam, says, "Networks are very sensitive to matters of taste. It's very subjective and often the three networks give three different opinions." Perhaps the storyboard portrays a woman in a dress cut lower than the network feels is acceptable; agency and network might work out a compromise in which the agency agrees to run the spot only after 9:00 P.M.

Dick Walburger, of DFS/Dorland, recalls a commercial for an over-the-counter cold remedy in which an older, mature couple was shown in bed. The networks would not allow both the man and the woman to be shown under the covers, so the storyboard was redrawn with the man on top of the bed. In the next go-around, the networks noticed that the woman's hands were visible and insisted that she wear a wedding ring.

Final approval from the networks, especially concerning matters of taste, is always subject to their seeing the finished spot. "Sometimes," says Nelson, "they even say, 'We're not quite sure how this is going to look in final form and we are cautioning you.'"

A few seasons ago, Anne Klein produced a thirty-second spot to announce a new fragrance. In it, a man and woman enter a city apartment in what appears to be the afternoon. The woman throws off her coat, removes her earrings, unbuttons a single button near the top of her blouse, and applies some perfume. The man comes over to her and brushes against her hair. Although innocuous in storyboard form, when NBC saw the finished spot, they refused to air it (although CBS and ABC did).

Network challenges do not involve just sexual innuendo and issues of taste. In the winter of 1986, Lowe Marshalk created "The Deficit Trials" for its client, W. R. Grace & Company. The spot featured a trial in which pale and ragged children were shown questioning an older man about why his generation had failed to reduce the deficit. The commercial was powerful as it graphically symbolized the consequences of long-term deficit spending.

The networks found the spot intimidating. Citing policies against running commercials that take a stand on public issues, they refused to allow "The Deficit Trials" to air over national television. However, on August 21, 1986, the spot was shown over almost 150 independent stations. The Association of Independent Television Stations had donated time worth approximately $250,000 in order for the spot to be aired.

Even when a spot is cleared for network broadcast, however, it can still be challenged. Once the commercial appears, consumers and competitors see it and may bring action either in civil court, through the National Advertising Division (NAD) of the Better Business Bureau, or the FTC. Agencies and clients almost always genuinely try to avoid creating advertising that can be challenged. The process of defending an ad is time-consuming and expensive, deflecting energies away from the real business at hand.

An advertiser can respond to a challenge simply by discontinuing the advertising, as did Frank Perdue when Perdue Farms was challenged for running an ad that claimed: "Golden yellow is the natural color of a chicken. Give it cheaper feed. Put it in a house with poor ventilation, it can lose some of that color. And if it ever gets sick, it'll lose still more of that nice yellow color. So don't ask why my chickens are so yellow. Wonder why some chickens are so white." Perdue first agreed to share substantiating material with the NAD but later decided simply to discontinue the advertising.

However, the Quaker Oats Company, which was challenged by B & M beans for claiming that its Van Camp's Baked Beans beat B & M's in taste tests, was able to provide test results to justify the claim. Not so fortunate, in one of the funnier claim disputes, was the Carnation Company, which touted its New Breed dog food as "the best-tasting dog food in a bag." Said the NAD: One cannot make claims on behalf of consumers who cannot make them for themselves.

American Home Products got into trouble over "net impression," one of advertising's murkier areas, in which an advertisement need not actually make an untruthful statement or claim to be considered deceptive. If the consumer picks up or perceives a misleading message from the advertisement, the spot is unacceptable. In this case, Johnson & Johnson, the manufacturer of Tylenol, sued American Home Products over an Anacin commercial. Johnson & Johnson stated that the way in which Anacin was advertised as superior in reducing inflammation led consumers to believe that it was also the most effective pain reliever available. Johnson & Johnson submitted research showing that people who viewed the commercial were convinced that Anacin was better in every way, although the truth was and is that reducing inflammation and relieving pain are two different issues. The case went to court, and American Home Products was told to stop airing the commercial. The court agreed that even though the commercial didn't say that Anacin was a superior pain reliever to Tylenol, consumers viewing the spot were left with that impression.

11

International

With the advertising business growing faster abroad than in the United States, U.S. agencies are increasingly active internationally. Even China now has a full-service, Western-style agency based in Beijing that opened in June 1986. The nation's first, the agency is staffed by writers, producers, account managers, researchers, and art directors, and is the result of a joint venture with Young & Rubicam. This international growth has given birth to a new breed of advertising professional, often called a "multinational," or, in a word coined by the industry monthly *Madison Avenue* to describe roving writer/art director creative teams, the "globoutique."

Often "on the road," which might include extended layovers at both sophisticated European capitals and out-of-the-way outposts, the multinational works with local agencies abroad to develop advertising that can transcend national boundaries while reflecting each nation's unique culture. As a roving creative-at-large, a multinational might spend a month in Taiwan gathering information on which to base a new campaign for its airline, six weeks in India organizing production for a soft-drink spot and, in between, four days in Lugano, Switzerland, meeting with the creative directors of his agency's international offices.

A look at some figures explains this relatively recent advertising phenomenon. According to *Madison Avenue*, the top twenty-five U.S.-based multinational corporations derive over 50 percent of their profits from overseas business.

ADWEEK reports that worldwide, businesses spent $150 billion advertising their products. Although more than half of that $150 billion was spent on advertising within the United States, American agencies are finding it increasingly profitable to extend their networks overseas. They either open offices abroad, buy existing foreign agencies, or merge with agencies in other countries.

These networks are extensive. In 1899 J. Walter Thompson opened an office in Great Britain, the first American agency to open a foreign office. Today, in addition to its twenty-one U.S. branch offices, Thompson has 135 advertising agencies in forty countries, including such diverse locations as Amsterdam, Brussels, London, Vienna, Zurich, Madrid, Paris, Copenhagen, Frankfurt, Milan, Bogotá, Mexico City, Lima, Buenos Aires, São Paulo, Santiago, Caracas, Hong Kong, Bangkok, Jakarta, Manila, Tokyo, Sydney, Kuala Lumpur, Seoul, Wellington, Colombo, Cape Town, and Singapore. *Advertising Age* reported that in 1984 Thompson's overseas billings were $1.25 billion, a figure amounting to 46.1 percent of its total billings of $2.7 billion.

Multinational clients are increasingly creating unified markets for their products. In what is called *global/multina-*

tional advertising, ads created by a single agency use the same advertising strategy—the same imagery and tone—throughout the world to market products. Probably the best-known examples of global advertising have been done for Coca-Cola, Levi Strauss, and Marlboro cigarettes.

Although the same creative strategy is used to market many multinational brands and services, the actual advertising material is frequently adapted from country to country, in order to reflect particular cultural differences. For instance, to introduce its EXG line of Scotch videocassettes, 3M used a single commercial that aired in English, Japanese, German, Spanish, and Italian markets. Research showed that people in each country were most concerned about color reproduction when purchasing videocassettes. Therefore, the spot emphasized vibrant and strong colors. However, Grey creatives used different music and copy in each market in order to appeal to local taste and traditions; the copy used in Germany stressed technology, whereas in Japan, where consumers are more visual, copy was pared down to a minimum. Even Trivial Pursuit went global with a $1.2 million campaign that used the same strategy throughout Europe, featuring photographs or caricatures of political leaders in each of the game's European markets playing Trivial Pursuit.

Saatchi & Saatchi, now the largest advertising agency in the world, stated in its 1984 annual report that an agency's goal must be "to find a real advertising idea so deep in its appeal that it can transcend national borders previously thought inviolate." In practical application, the agency's best-known example of this is the British Airways "Manhattan Landing" commercial, which shows the island of Manhattan coming in for a landing at London's Heathrow Airport. The ninety-second spot was shown in forty-six countries unchanged except for the voice-over. So successful was the spot, according to *ADWEEK*, that British Airways showed a 106 percent increase in sales.

As multinational businesses consolidate marketing and advertising capabilities, decision making is centralized. Whereas local advertising agencies used to get business from the local facility of an international company, centralization means that these businesses use fewer local advertising agencies, awarding more of their business to a few. For example, in 1984 Eastman Kodak reduced the number of agencies it used to promote its products from thirty-five to two.

Global marketing makes it difficult for small agencies to keep clients when these clients grow and begin to sell products and services abroad. In order to stay competitive, it is now practically an imperative for a national advertising agency to add international capabilities to the list of services it can offer its clients. In 1986 the award-winning Minneapolis-based Fallon McElligott Rice sold a 75 percent share of its agency to New York–based Scali, McCabe, Sloves. Although Fallon McElligott Rice partners obviously benefited financially from this union, the long-term benefit to the agency is access to Scali offices in Australia, France, England, Germany, Brazil, Mexico, and Canada, which will allow the smaller agency to service its growing roster of clients with overseas marketing needs.

Moral issues come into play more often internationally than in the United States. In 1984 the United Nations Conference on Trade and Development called for measures that would decrease the "acceptance of long-established brand names" internationally. This was prompted by the fact that businesses in the developing and poorer nations cannot begin to compete in their local marketplaces, to say nothing of the world market, when pitted against internationally marketed and recognizable products.

Although most Western nations have stringent regulations that govern advertising, many nations—particularly third-world and developing nations—have minimal advertising restrictions. There has long been concern about U.S. drug companies that market and advertise abroad drugs that have been banned in the United States, as well as the indiscriminate promotion of products like cigarettes.

Most agencies are committed to staffing their international branches with local advertising professionals, but U.S.-based headquarters are increasingly involved in international operations. There are expanding opportunities for skilled multinational creatives with account experience, and a relatively new career track is opening up.

David Herzbrun and Don Blauweiss, now at Saatchi & Saatchi but longtime veterans of Doyle Dane Bernbach, pioneered the "globoutique" concept while working on international business at DDB. Before moving to Saatchi & Saatchi, the copywriter/art director team talked about their work, describing themselves—according to Blauweiss—as "creative commandos," on call to go anywhere. When the team assumed international responsibilities, it was, says Blauweiss, "the job that I had designed for myself in my own mind but never knew existed."

As creative consultants, the Herzbrun/Blauweiss team was available to all of DDB's foreign agencies. They filled in when there were temporary creative staffing problems and, when asked, offered advice and creative direction for local campaigns. Together with local agencies, Herzbrun and Blauweiss created global/multinational advertising campaigns, capable of appealing to diverse cultures yet with uniformity and common strategy.

Until recently, few agencies offered international clients the kind of creative services that Herzbrun and Blauweiss performed while at DDB. Obviously recent agency mergers arranged, in part, to assure clients' advertising capabilities overseas are responsible for the growth of multinational career opportunities. But, as Blauweiss points out, there are not many creatives with a combination of language skills, administrative experience, and international employment background.

Getting local agencies to call on the Blauweiss/Herzbrun team initially wasn't easy. "A lot of the local agencies," says Herzbrun, "saw us as competition instead of help. They are now calling on us more and more, whereas a year and a half ago, we often had to wedge ourselves into situations." Today local agencies are more eager to use the team, realizing that in any multinational situation, even if only two countries are involved, it often helps to have the fresh perspective of someone who is not immersed in local culture.

Herzbrun relates a fairly typical situation: "We were called by the head of the Belgium office to help develop a pitch for Quick, a hamburger chain with headquarters in Belgium, which has more outlets than McDonald's does in Europe but hardly any mind awareness. Whenever there is a multinational campaign in the sense of a single theme that must work in more than one country, we usually get involved.

"Basically, Quick was saying: 'Here we are, the largest hamburger chain in Belgium, and nobody knows about us. We are the largest in France and nobody knows about us. We are starting to do business in Germany, England, and Italy, and we intend to expand throughout Europe.' Here you have five countries with totally different marketing situations. We want to create awareness and get people to start noticing and thinking about this particular chain."

To compound the marketing problem, Belgium is a country with two distinct cultures, one French and the other

Flemish. The campaign had to speak to both. Yet not only are the languages different, but each group is apt to respond to a different tone. This is not an atypical situation abroad. There are frequently differences in the way a single product must be advertised within the same country.

Talking about the development of the Quick campaign, Herzbrun continues, "I am a copywriter, but when working internationally, I come up with ideas and concepts that don't depend upon language. There is no idea in the world that can't be communicated, but you must be careful about getting into local references, puns, and colloquialisms. They can't be translated.

"We decided to base the campaign upon a hamburger-gap concept. But we had to be careful about even using the word 'gap' in developing the concept for the Quick campaign. You can't translate it into another language and have it work. It's an idea—a concept—and because it is a strong one, it will work. But you must learn to think nonverbally when working internationally.

"We decided that we would pretend that America is really concerned that Europe is pulling ahead in hamburgers. We'll do clips of Reagan talking with subtitles in French, Flemish, and all the other languages. It will look like authentic newsreel footage and the tone will be affectionate and cute. We will produce the commercials centrally but then local agencies in each country will take over, following the same theme. For instance, the French agency will do voice-overs or subtitles on the commercials and all the print that must be colloquial, including outdoor and newspapers."

In most countries, television is government-supported, with limitations on the amount of paid advertising that can be broadcast over the air waves. Until recently, advertisers who wanted to take advantage of the limited time available for television advertising often had to book commercial time a year in advance. According to *Advertising Age*, those stations that did accept television advertising tended to allow fewer than sixty minutes of advertising per day—as compared with an average of 540 minutes in the United States. However, these networks are now accepting more ads. There are also more privately owned stations, as well as a proliferation of satellite-beamed cable television channels throughout Europe. These developments are increasing the already growing tendency of businesses to consolidate and centralize their advertising. Since television production is so expensive, clients seek agencies that have the capabilities to create single commercials that can work across national boundaries.

Blauweiss talks about a project he and Herzbrun did for Doyle Dane Bernbach's office in Spain. "Our Madrid office asked us to help pitch the Spanish Government Tourist Office. They wanted to develop an international campaign that would run in international magazines such as the international editions of *Time, Newsweek,* the *Herald Tribune,* the *Financial Times,* and *National Geographic.*

"People tend to think of Spain as a cheap vacation place with plenty of sun but not too much culture. We were trying to get people to understand that, in addition to sun and beaches, Spain has a diverse culture, a history, and a wonderful cuisine. But we had different audiences. Northern Europeans, who have a deep and rich culture of their own, are not going to have the same attraction to cultural events in Spain that an American might. These people are primarily interested in the sun. But we didn't want to sell Spain on sun alone.

"Together with the local agency, we developed the strategy. We knew whom we wanted to reach and speak to, as

172

opposed to whom we used to speak to. We all discussed the proper tone and the media that would be necessary to reach those we wanted to attract. We decided to use the tag line 'Everything under the sun' in all of the ads.

"The line worked very well in English but when it came time to extend the campaign and use it in different languages, it didn't always work. The 'Everything under the sun' line works in Dutch and German, but not in French or Italian. And to make things even more complicated, in Italy the line 'Your place in the sun' had been used by Mussolini after he conquered Ethiopia—a typical example of what can happen when you start translating from one language to another."

This is not an uncommon problem. A classic example occurred when Chevrolet introduced the Nova, a new automobile, in Puerto Rico. *No va* means "doesn't go" in Spanish—not a good name for an automobile. In another situation, Saatchi & Saatchi/Compton was planning to launch a shampoo in Canada called Pert. Fortunately, however, before advertising appeared, it was discovered that *perte* in French Canada means "loss," not an association an advertiser wants his audience to make with a hair product. The shampoo was renamed Prêt, which in French means "ready." And when, in Belgium and the Netherlands, General Motors proclaimed "Body by Fisher" while advertising the company that builds its cars' interiors, the translation in Flemish was "Corpse by Fisher."

The Herzbrun/Blauweiss team and other multinational creatives often see something new and exciting in what, to a local, might be ordinary and run-of-the-mill. Although they are at work, Blauweiss and Herzbrun are also tourists. Herzbrun talks of an experience that, while exciting for any visitor, provided the basis for a successful ad. "One midnight," he says, "as we were driving back to Madrid, we happened on a fiesta, the Fiesta San Juan. It wasn't a glamorous fiesta, just an ordinary people's festival. Don doesn't usually do the photography for ads, but he got some wonderful pictures.

"When we came back and told the Madrid office that we had taken pictures and wanted to do an ad on the Fiesta San Juan, they said, 'You don't want to do that. It's nothing special.'

"But it gave us the hook to use in dealing with nightlife. The ad ran with copy that said, 'Come dance with us: It's one o'clock in the morning in this little village. Can you imagine what's happening in the cities?' But, more than that, this ad shows that something can happen to you if you go to Spain. It conveys a feeling of promise and possibility. You can get involved and be more than an outsider.

"What it really comes down to is that people are people. They respond to the same things and want the same things— food, shelter, love, security. In all places, when people are amused, they laugh, and when they are unhappy, they cry. The only thing that is different is pure logic and therefore logic will hardly ever work from country to country. The real motivations are supracultural—and if you draw upon them, you will be understood."

Appendix
Getting a Job in Advertising

As in most so-called glamour professions, entry-level positions in advertising are not easy to come by. But with organization and motivation, serious job seekers will find work. And one of the real pluses of the advertising business is that once your foot is in the door, advancement usually comes rapidly. Newcomers have the opportunity to prove themselves quickly.

The preceding chapters contained information specific to individual agency departments. Below are some general tips and resources applicable to anyone who is interested in a career in advertising.

1. Be specific. Don't simply look for "a job in advertising." Do research. Create a network. Speak to friends, relatives, and school alumni contacts. Check bookstores and libraries for up-to-date career publications and visit career information centers in public and school libraries.

Before embarking on a job search, it is important to get a feel for the business of advertising and to decide which area best suits you and for which you are best qualified.

For up-to-date information about the advertising business, the following publications are essential reading:

Advertising Age
740 Rush Street
Chicago, Illinois 60611-2591
(312) 649-5200

ADWEEK
A S M Communications, Inc.
820 Second Avenue
New York, New York 10017
(212) 661-8080

Both of these are weekly publications that provide extensive coverage of agencies, clients, and the advertising business. In addition, both contain special features and report on specific facets of advertising such as direct marketing and creative trends. Both *Advertising Age* and *ADWEEK* are available by subscription, in many libraries, and at certain newsstands.

Madison Avenue
Madison Avenue Publishing Corporation
369 Lexington Avenue
New York, New York 10017
(212) 972-0600

This is a monthly magazine that contains features on advertising trends, personalities, and specific advertising campaigns.

The *New York Times* runs a daily column on advertising that contains current advertising news and examines trends.

2. Decide what type of agency you wish to work in. Consider agency location, size, specialty, and types of accounts. Below are two essential publications.

> *Standard Directory of Advertising Agencies*
> National Register Publishing Co., Inc.
> 3004 Glenview Road
> Wilmette, Illinois 60091
> (312) 256-6067

More commonly called the "Agency Red Book," this directory lists over four thousand agencies and includes the names of key personnel, addresses of branch offices, and lists major accounts. It is probably the single most important reference tool. The "Red Book" is published three times a year and supplements are published monthly. It is available at most libraries.

> *Standard Directory of Advertisers*
> National Register Publishing Co., Inc.
> 3004 Glenview Road
> Wilmette, Illinois 60091
> (312) 256-6067

This companion volume lists more than 17,000 advertisers, with names of key personnel and their advertising agencies.

3. Consult a comprehensive guide to organizing a job search in advertising. The best such guide is the *Adver-*

tising Career Directory, which contains information on résumé preparation and interview strategies and lists agencies with internship and training programs as well as colleges with advertising majors. It is available in many libraries and from the publisher ($24.95, plus $3.50 for shipping).

> *Advertising Career Directory*
> Career Publishing Corp.
> 505 Fifth Avenue
> New York, New York 10017
> (800) 835-2246

Although there are recruitment agencies that specialize in placing people in advertising positions, you will find that they do not usually handle entry-level jobs. Instead, beginners must go directly to the ad agencies in which they are interested. Always send your résumé and cover letter to the person who actually does the hiring. Contact department heads such as the creative director, the head of media planning, or the director of research.

Always call before sending résumés and letters of inquiry to make sure that you have the person's correct name and title. Even though the "Red Book" and other directories are regularly updated, they are not infallible, particularly since people frequently change positions and agencies.

Be sure to follow up after you have made the initial contact. You shouldn't take it personally but it is highly unlikely that a busy media director or production head will get back to you. You will have to take the initiative.

The following organizations are good sources of advertising information:

Advertising Women of New York
153 East 57th Street
New York, New York 10022
(212) 593-1950

Advertising Women of New York (AWNY) is a professional organization of approximately eight hundred women in executive positions in the communications industry, including advertising, research, marketing, merchandising, promotion, public relations, and media. AWNY conducts seminars and luncheon programs and an annual career conference for college students interested in advertising and communications.

American Advertising Federation
1400 K Street, Suite 1000
Washington, D.C. 20005
(212) 898-0089

The American Advertising Federation's Advertising Educational Foundation is a source of career-related literature.

American Association of Advertising Agencies
666 Third Avenue
New York, New York 10017
(212) 682-2500

The AAAA—the 4 A's—is the largest and most prestigious advertising association, to which all the major agencies belong. It publishes several guides to advertising careers.

Art Directors Club
488 Madison Avenue
New York, New York 10022
(212) 838-8140

This is a trade organization for graphic-arts professionals that develops educational programs as well. The Portfolio Review program offers aspiring art directors the opportunity for one-on-one counseling and advice from professionals in the field.

Association of National Advertisers
155 East 44th Street
New York, New York 10017
(212) 697-5950

The ANA is a client organization that publishes reports, studies, and books on all phases of advertising and marketing. Write for a free listing of ANA publications.

Business/Professional Advertising Association
205 East 42nd Street
New York, New York 10017
(212) 661-0222

With a membership ranging from those involved in advertising and marketing to business and industry professionals, the B/PAA has student chapters and publishes literature of interest to someone considering business-to-business communication.

Direct Mail/Marketing Association
66 East 43rd Street
New York, New York 10017
(212) 689-4977

The Direct Mail/Marketing Association's Educational Foundation administers a Summer Internship Program, Career

Day Program, and a résumé-forwarding service, and also publishes career-related literature.

The One Club
251 East 50th Street
New York, New York 10022
(212) 935-0121

An organization for art directors and copywriters, the One Club encourages student memberships and administers several educational programs including counseling (a thirty-minute career-counseling session with a professional in the field), a portfolio review, and regular seminars and workshops. In addition, there is a résumé-forwarding service in which student résumés are forwarded to employers who have entry-level opportunities.

The Society of Illustrators
128 East 63rd Street
New York, New York 10021
(212) 838-2560

The organization offers career seminars and portfolio review and publishes a booklet, *Society of Illustrators' Career Guidance in Illustration and Graphic Design,* which offers advice on portfolio preparation.

Index

183